Youth: Reflection of Universe

OrangeBooks Publication

Smriti Nagar, Bhilai, Chhattisgarh - 490020

Website: **www.orangebooks.in**

First Edition, 2020

ISBN: 978-93-90169-01-6

Printed in India

Youth:
Reflection of Universe

Pankaj Jagannath Jayswal

OrangeBooks Publication
www.orangebooks.in

ACKNOWLEDGEMENT

I first of all thank Lord Ganesh for showering his abundant grace upon me to author this book.

I would like to express my sense of indebtedness to all spiritual masters for offering abundant knowledge and ability to see the potentials for the betterment of society.

I would like to thank My Late father Shri Jagannath V. Jayswal for his blessings all the time. I would like to thank my mother, my son, In laws, siblings and relatives for their continued support and blessings.

I would like to thank my wife Priyanka for encouraging me to write this book and review of Hindi version of this book. I would like to express special thanks to my daughter Kritika for review and advise on many topics.

My sincere gratitude for Shri Pranendra Nath Mishra, Author and retired government officer, without whom translating this book in Hindi was impossible.

I would like to express my deep sense of gratitude towards my students and friends for believing me and encouraging me time to time.

Special thanks to OrangeBooks Publication and whole team for the efforts put even during lockdown due to COVID-19.

I want to thank everyone who ever uttered something positive to me or taught me something. I heard it all, and it meant something.

May the Lord Ganesh bless all of you with lot of happiness, fulfilled life.

INDEX

INTRODUCTION

We, human beings are blessed with vast intellect, vast memory and huge ego to drive ourselves to betterment and achieve higher goals in life. The ultimate purpose of everything you do is to achieve happiness and peace of mind.

However, nobody teach us how to manage our mind, and make effective use of intellect to achieve higher self, well utilize our memory and put checks on our ego.

Ultimately, most of the people mess up with their life and even though they have all the resources needed to fulfill their desires.

All over the world, majority of youths now a day are confused, stressed, frustrated, addicted on drugs, directionless, depressed, suffering anxiety, violent and never the less full of negative energies. You must have noticed these traits among different people in society. I am not stating that everyone has such problem but its commonly noticeable in today's generation.

The question is, "Are they bad?" Don't they have competence to live a good, eloquent and joyful life??

Answer to all such undesirable questions is big "NO".

Let us open the doorway of our minds and find out the root cause behind all these issues which are grappling around our modern day youths.

Education system is designed in such a way that, we do not emphasis on fundamental aspects like:

- Pressure, challenges and difficulties are part of our life and how to manage them with ease of mind and smartness
- How to handle stress and stressful state of affairs
- How to manage mind in different situations to achieve higher goals
- How to check ego and work on it
- How to clean our memory of unwanted stuff, negativity and worst experiences
- How to maintain physical health
- How to maintain environment
- How to express emotions, feelings in different situation with ease
- How great people in the past and present achieved success with lot of difficulties, what was/is special in them
- How to be a great leader with commitment, passion, belongingness, perseverance, high energy with positive attitude
- Love and affection towards society, nation and environmental factors (Biotic and abiotic)
- Love and respect oneself to see good in every action one does
- What is life and real purpose of life

As a counselor and close association with youths/students, I realized that today's generation has great potential, capabilities, but somehow our education system, teachers, parents and overall society have changed its priorities, methods, systems towards youth causing uneasiness among them leading to unwanted traits mentioned above.

My intention is not just to highlight the negative aspects, but the root cause of it. And by which ways we as a parent, teacher, society can overcome these issues and bring positivity in our youths. I have personally experienced that our youths are very receptive to positive changes, that's why I am successful in bringing many of them back to normal life from their miserable life with full of anxieties, Suicidal tendencies, drug addiction, exam fear and many more dreadful aspects.

EDUCATION AND MIND

> **"Education is the most powerful weapon, which you can use to change the world."**
>
> **—Nelson Mandela**

In USA a well-known university conducted a survey among successful students in various field to find out the causes behind their success. It was surprising to note that, whatever they have achieved academically (Doctor, Engineer, Lawyer, science graduate, Chartered accountants, MBA or any other degree...) contributed just 13% and the remaining 87% was "Life Management"

And neither school nor family teach us the "Life Management".

What is "Life Management"??

It means handling ourselves in different circumstances that includes managing ups and downs in life, stressful situations, anger and fear, material and spiritual growth by ethical means. Unfortunately, most of us have never been taught in a right manner by any faculties of the society.

The only emphasis of most of the parents and schools is to secure good grades/marks in the exam and on accomplishing the formal education. We never give significance to various crucial aspects of life like managing the mind, character building, building positive attitude, maintain equanimity in all situations, right thinking and actions towards society and country. As a result, it become difficult for lot of people in society to handle success in an effective way for a long span. At the same time, failures are even more difficult to handle causing mental issues, substantial fall in self-confidence, loss of all hope.

Mind management is a intricate subject, when we encounter success, it elevates our EGO, takes us away from the subtle reality, affecting our relationship with our near and dear ones. You must have experienced that "Success is directly proportional to criticism", more you are successful, more you will be criticized. Many people in society will try to put you down by making insults, will slur on your character and so on. if mind is feeble then it will be difficult to sustain with success for a longer period of time. So, the significant question is, "how to handle constructive and destructive criticism"?

Will discuss it in upcoming chapters.

> *"Success is never final, and failure is never fatal. It's courage that counts."*
>
> *It is your state of mind (weak or strong) decides the course of action, a weak mind will never channelize your energy for higher purposeful goals, and strong mind will always look for different opportunities in difficult situations with joy to reach higher goals.*

Since childhood, our mind is nurtured by our predecessors in such a way, that challenges, difficulties, problems are defined as not a good aspect, keep away from complex situations and a false notion is created in our mind that, 'only academic studies can keep you protected from difficult circumstances, so study hard'. Let me clear you that primarily education/studies is significant, don't ignore it; but mentioning that, 'it will rest hitches of life forever is a big joke'.

Let them understand life is a blend of good and bad, right and wrong, happiness and sadness, positives and negatives, hero and villain, success and failure, opportunities and difficulties, peace and disturbance, everything is complimentary. The problem is that we always ensure to put in subtle mind that one part of life which we face is good and other part is bad and can be avoided. How can we avoid the part which brings out inner potentials which we have but never realized, makes us strong, experienced, makes us creative, innovative, shows how important is our life and improves our managing skills? You will agree that we learn to live life only after we face difficulties in life.

> *Ups and downs in life are very important to keep us going because a straight line even in an ECG means we are not live.*
>
> *-Sri Ratan Tata*

The Indecisive Frog

Once upon a time, A frog fell in a vessel of the hot water. The water was still on a gas stove. The frog still did not try to jump out of the vessel, instead just stayed in it. As the temperature of the water started to rise, the frog managed to adjust its body temperature accordingly. As the water started to reach the boiling point, the frog was no longer able to keep up and manage its body temperature according to the temperature of water.

The frog tried to jump out of the vessel but with water temperature reaching its boiling point, the frog was not able to bear it and couldn't make it. What was the reason that a frog couldn't make it? Will you blame the hot water for this?

Moral of the Story:

Sometimes in life, things don't happen the way we want them to be. But no matter how unhappy we are because of the situation, it's important to come in to action, so we can face the problem ahead. The frog in the story was indecisive and stubborn. Instead of jumping out of the water right away, he waited until he could no longer bear the heat, die in the process. Distinguishing between when to adjust and when not, and taking appropriate action before it's too late is certainly very crucial.

It's important to act proactively and decisively in difficult situation; keeping yourself aware and alert to take the right decision at right moment is most crucial. Again this will be only possible, if we have a strong mind.

Strong mind is decisive and alert.

Let the child learn the art of celebrating every difficulty they encounter. It means they must see all situations with equanimity. We have experienced that good times look short as compare with hard times. Harsh situations look never ending. Why is this happen? We resist the bad times in realm of intellect, so non-acceptance on level of one's mind, creates impression that it is ever lasting. And we keep on thinking about that all the time. However, this is not so in real life.

How to identify a weak mind: -

1. Only believes in short term pleasure.
2. Don't believe in hard work, tries to find shortcut.
3. Though the path chosen is wrong but want to get it done to please his mind.
4. Procrastinate the work in hand, laziness.
5. Lack of Commitment to any work/project/activity.
6. Blame others for own inactions.
7. Excuses and complaining attitude for no reason.
8. Never committed to higher goal, changes goals quite often to find out escape route.
9. Strongly believes in short term pleasures like physical/sexual attraction, drug addiction.
10. No discipline for important goals.
11. Easily gets distracted.
12. Waste major time on activities which are irrelevant, non-essential like video games.
13. Focuses more on negatives than positives.
14. Avoids tough situations, example: test papers.
15. Lack of confidence and motivation.
16. Fear of rejection.
17. Long term, chances of going into depression and developing suicidal tendencies.
18. Weak Emotionally.

19. It's not easy to convert weak mind to strong one, but it's also not impossible. We will see how to make

strong mind in coming chapters, and we will also go through celebrities who have successfully turned their fortunes.

How to identify a strong mind: -

1. Always plans and work for short and long term goals.
2. Always welcomes challenges.
3. Always looks for opportunities in difficult situation.
4. Always treats failure as steppingstone to success.
5. Focused, confident.
6. Innovative, creative.
7. Focuses more on positives than negatives.
8. Disciplined, creates positive atmosphere.
9. Reading habit, always improves knowledge and skills.
10. Caring and sharing.
11. Loves to be ethical.
12. Believes in team spirit.
13. Believes in service to society and country.
14. Develops leadership qualities.
15. Passionate about work/hobbies/project.
16. Believes in present moment.
17. Emotionally balanced.

Everyone would love to be recognized with these qualities.

How to be Mentally strong

- Never give up after your first failure
- Never waste energy on things you can't control
- Never dwell in the past
- Never let others influence your emotions

Belief in Yourself

A gentleman was walking through an elephant camp, and he spotted that the elephants weren't being kept in cages or held using chains.

All that was holding them back from escaping the camp, was a small piece of rope tied to one of their legs.

As the man gazed upon the elephants, he was completely confused as to why the elephants didn't just use their strength to break the rope and escape the camp. They could easily have done so, but instead, they didn't try to at all.

Curious and wanting to know the answer, he asked a trainer nearby why the elephants were just standing there and never tried to escape.

The trainer replied, "when they are very young and much smaller, we use the same size rope to tie them and, at that age, it's enough to hold them. As they grow up, they are conditioned to believe they cannot break away. They believe the rope can still hold them, so they never try to break free." The only reason that the elephants weren't breaking free and escaping from the camp was that over time they adopted the belief that it just wasn't possible.

Moral of the story:

No matter how much the world tries to hold you back, always endure with the belief that, what you want to achieve is possible. Believing that, you could be successful is the most important step to become successful.

Success is not measured by the heights one attains, but by the obstacles one overcomes in its attainment.

"Study hard, no matter if it seems impossible, no matter if it takes time, no matter if you have to be up all night, just remember that the feeling of success is the best thing in the entire world."

Ways Of Parenting

> **"Encourage and support your kids because children are apt to live up to what you believe of them".**

Parents always have unconditional love for their kids. They want to give everything to their child, no matter they can afford it or not. They do hard work without expecting anything in return. They want to see their child as good citizen, successful in life, ethical, healthy.

But it doesn't seem to happen with everyone. What are the causes? Let's discuss...

Kids are like a mirror; what they see and hear they do. Be a good reflection of them.

1. Parents expectations are based on their unfulfilled desires, so they want their children to accomplish their unresolved wishes/desires, no matter whether their child desires those too or not.
2. Parents wants to see their child better than children in neighborhood and far better than their relatives. Denying the _UNIQUENESS_ of every child and endeavoring to neglect that side of the child.
3. Few parents loves to vigorously inculcate their notions and prejudices about almost everything, which were based on their past experiences.
4. Few parents either overestimate or underestimate the capabilities of a child.
5. Many parents are misled by nonsense they get on internet and social media.
6. Financial and Health issues.

7. Many parents likes to take control of their child's freedom.
8. Illiteracy, social backwardness.

So, what actions parent need to take??

*   Nothing wrong in expecting from a child, but it is miserable to expect from your child when he/she is just a foetus or a toddler, it is the most damaging for a child's future. In lieu of expectation, start building their foundational aspects. Two to six years of age is very crucial for shaping up the child's mind, develop intellect, enlighten them with right values. During childhood, a child learns a lot of new concepts, develops thinking patterns by observing parents, relatives, friends and surrounding.

*   Encourage them to do anything creative while remaining playful and joyous. Involve them in logical games and activities. In their growth phase, let them learn to respect elders and nature, caring and sharing, teach them the importance of being ethical.

Children learn more from what you are than what you teach.

*   Researches on the child behavior shows that, most of the time we speak or instruct child negatively. This is how we program their mindset and afterwards, we expect them to listen and fulfil our wishes.

A negative mindset cannot create anything positive. Positive talk is all we needed even when we give them feedback on something not done right. Positive mindset not only channelise the energy for our upliftment, but also spreads positivity around us.

A positive mindset can do miracles, can make impossible, possible. So, it is utmost important to develop a positive self-talk.

Thinking Out of the Box
(Positive Thinking)

In a small British town, hundreds of years ago, a small business owner owed a large sum of money to a loan-shark. The loan-shark was a very old, unattractive looking guy that just so happened to fancy the businessman's daughter.

He decided to offer the businessman a deal that would completely wipe out the debt he owed him. However, the catch was that we would only wipe out the debt if he could marry the businessman's daughter. This proposal was met with a look of disgust.

The loan-shark said that he would place two pebbles into a bag, one white and one black.

The daughter would then have to reach into the bag and pick out a pebble. If it was black, the debt would be wiped, and the loan-shark would then marry her. If it was white, the debt would also be wiped, but the daughter wouldn't have to marry the loan-shark. Standing on a pebble-strewn path in the businessman's garden, the loan-shark bent over and picked up two pebbles. Whilst he was picking them up, the daughter noticed that he'd picked up two black pebbles and placed them both into the bag.

He then asked the daughter to reach into the bag and pick one.

The daughter naturally had three choices as to what she could have done:

- Refuse to pick a pebble from the bag.
- Take both pebbles out of the bag and expose the loan-shark for cheating.
- Pick a pebble from the bag fully well knowing it was black and sacrifice herself for her father's freedom.

She drew out a pebble from the bag, and before looking at it 'accidentally' dropped it into the midst of the other pebbles. She said to the loan-shark, "Oh, how clumsy of me. Never mind, if you investigate the bag for the one that is left, you will be able to tell which pebble I picked."

The pebble left in the bag is obviously black and seeing as the loan-shark didn't want to be exposed, he had to play along as if the pebble the daughter dropped was white and clear her father's debt.

Moral of the story:

It's always possible to overcome a tough situation through positive and out of the box thinking.

- Criticism is good, but kind of criticism we make matters a lot. Constructive criticism is always a best practice to follow. You are bang on the point you want to make and at the same time you shouldn't hurt the sentiments of a child. Whereas, destructive criticism makes bad impact on mindset of whom you criticize, affects relationship, hurts ego, bringing negativity and developing stubborn attitude. Never scold or criticize in front of your child friends and relatives. Its hurt them badly. If they have made some mistake and its need to be addressed, then first control your anger for a moment and scold in solitary, and let him/her know that you could scold in front of their friends, but you have honor his/her self-respect and wants a positive change.

- Never give harsh punishment to the child for the mistakes, they will become intolerant and violent with others for small mistake, that is what they learned from you. It's better to handle every situation with calm mind without getting stressed or panicked whenever you are with them, it will program their mind subtly the same way, will help them to lead a better life. Your aggressive nature will bring the same quality in their behavior in difficult situations. Parent's actions and reactions to the various situations, incidents, events create deep impressions in their mind. Child keep watching closely to parents and teachers and imitate them in their life. So be careful, aware and alert.

"If you are not open to constructive criticism, then you are not truly open to growing as person"

"If you are not criticized, you may not be doing much that makes a difference"

"Accept both compliments and criticism. It takes sun and rain for a flower to grow"

The Foolish Monkey (Story for students)

It was a cold and silent night. The weather was freezing cold. A group of monkeys was on a tree. They were clinging to its branches. One of the monkeys said, "I wish we could find some fire. It will help us to keep warm."

Suddenly they noticed a flock of fireflies. One of the young monkeys thought it was fire. He caught a firefly. He put it under a dry leaf and started blowing at it. Some other monkeys also joined in his efforts.

In the meanwhile, a sparrow came flying to its nest, which was on the same tree the monkeys were sitting on. She noticed what they were doing. The sparrow laughed. She said, "Hey silly monkeys that is a firefly, not real fire. I think all of you should take shelter in a cave."

The monkeys did not listen to the sparrow. They continued to blow at the poor firefly.

After some time, the monkeys became very tired. Now they realized that what the sparrow had said was correct. They set free the firefly and moved to a nearby cave.

Moral of the Story:

While consistency is one of the most defining qualities of a good student, there's always something new to be learned every day! The monkeys in the story sure are consistent but their hard work didn't pay off because they refused to listen, at least initially. Always listen to your elders, they know better!

- Child doesn't need you whole day; they just need some quality time with you. Be 100% attentive when you spent time with them. Listen them 100%, have a conversation with eye to eye contact with full of love, fully submerged in conversation. Appreciate them in between, smile, laugh, have fun. Let them feel special, energetic and motivated. Teach them in silent and subtle manner to be happy and confident while giving 100% effort in studies/ activities/ games…

Let the child feel that you are part of their life.

Let them also realize the importance of physical, mental and social health. Encourage them to join you for little walks, Yoga, Pranayama, Meditation, exercise. This will help them work on health when they notice positive changes in lifestyle. Automatically, it will strengthen the mind, improve concentration, built up strong immunity system.

> ***"You either give 100 percent or you don't give at all"***
>
> ***"Don't put in half of the effort unless you are OKAY with half of the result."***

- Let them focus on both the aspects of life, Materialistic as well as Spiritual to bring balance in life along with peace of mind and see the bigger picture of life. Focusing only on materialistic life will lead to short term pleasures like sexual urge (lust) before right age, earning money through any means even though they are not legal ones and also leads to disturbed mind.

  Spiritual practices will pave way to see life with bigger dimensions with calm mind, to uplift materialistically. Success achieved with the help of both the aspects will be for longer term and will give real joy.

- Don't compare your child with their siblings or relatives, it creates a negative pressure on their mind. Comparison always brings a sense of jealousy, hatred against each other. Rather than improving performance, it only affects the performance and confidence. The child sees parents as enemies, stops listening and cooperation.

  Comparison should be done with child's own performance, if you see improvement, appreciate and encourage to do even better. If the performance is down, sit and discuss with them, how it can be improved, keep a track on the actions planned. It will surely be a win-win situation for parents as well as children.

- Let them know and be aware of good friends in life. Right friends lift each other and never distract each other from goal. Real friend will always help not only in good times but surely in bad times. If the performance, behavior is going down, time to change friends. A bad friend spoils life, sometimes encourages to do things which are socially evil and even drags towards drug addictions affecting health and overall life.

Being in a new surrounding with a new set of friends is indeed exciting if you're a student. But beware of the people who are just posing as your friend. In the same way, you must be supportive of your friends by standing by them in any situation.

- Don't give everything they demand immediately or in the first instance, it will develop a mindset that desires/demands are fulfilled without hard work, efforts, struggle. It will make them lazy, stubborn, arrogant, non-gratuitous, will take everything for granted, won't respect the hard work of parents. If situation arises where in parents won't be able to fulfil a wish even though fulfilled all earlier wishes, they will forget everything done before, they will keep on reminding themselves that their wish is not fulfilled, means parents don't love and are not with them. They become rebellious against parents.

Let them understand the importance of money, time and their elders. Nothing comes free; hard work, efforts are essential to achieve, gain anything worth in life.

- Many parents tend to impress child by divulging material facts like how much money they have in the bank for their child's future life, houses, lands, gold, silver. What happens, a child creates strong impressions in their mind that everything is done for them and they don't have to put efforts for living.

This creates a vicious circle around them, they put themselves in a comfort zone which starts creating fear in their mind, it degrades further by losing confidence, trust in oneself, lost attitude to take even calculated risk, these qualities either take them in depression over a time or they become stubborn, non-caring attitude, get into illegal activities, drug addiction, arrogant. They feel that whatever has been done by parents, it was their duty as they had given them birth. You might have noticed many such youth send their parents to orphanage.

- One more analysis says, child grown up by both parents does better than single parent. I am not saying anything wrong about single parent. Circumstances, untimely death of a spouse and some other reasons forces them to remain as single parent. Just want to share my experience with child having single parent. They generally want both parents in their life. It becomes difficult for them to answer friends, sometimes teachers, so it annoys them and makes them feel depressed.

Single parent is seen as bad in our society that is unfortunate, so the mindset of a child suffers a lot in daily life. I request parents, children must be their main priority, every couple in the universe has difference of opinion on any subject, issue and it is natural to have conflicts, arguments. They should respect each other's views, egos, give space to express each other freely. Sometimes, our ego overpowers our intellect, mind then our relationship and to the extend results in parting away. We need to think of children at that moment, how we are on the verge of destroying their life. Can we keep our egos aside and think about our lovely and loving kids and how best we can give them to be loved, respected by society?

"It's Not Whether You Get Knocked Down, It's Whether You Get Up."

Box Full of Kisses (Love)

Some time ago, a man punished his 3-year-old daughter for wasting a roll of gold wrapping paper. Money was tight and he became infuriated when the child tried to decorate a box to put under the Christmas tree.

Nevertheless, the little girl brought the gift to her father the next morning and said, "This is for you, Daddy."

The man became embarrassed by his overreaction earlier, but his rage continues when he saw that the box was empty. He yelled at her; "Don't you know, when you give someone a present, there is supposed to be something inside?"

The little girl looked up at him with tears in her eyes and cried, "Oh, Daddy, it's not empties at all. I blew kisses into the box. They're all for you, Daddy."

The father was crushed. He put his arms around his little girl, and he begged for her forgiveness.

Only a short time later, an accident took the life of the child.

Her father kept the gold box by his bed for many years and, whenever he was discouraged, he would take out an imaginary kiss and remember the love of the child who had put it there.

Moral of the story:

Love is the most precious gift in the world.

TEACHING METHODOLOGY

Numerous points which are applicable to parents, also applicable to teachers. Teachers have special place in developing the society and country. They are the backbone of our society, growth and success of child depends on teachers by almost 50%. Half of the future of a child is in the hands of teachers. They have a crucial role to play to uplift society through youngsters.

What are their responsibilities towards students?

They are: -

- Belongingness and responsibility are interconnected. If you have belongingness, then only you will take responsibility 100%. So, first thing, teachers should love and be passionate for their profession, it should not be mere formality for earning. If they feel school and students are part of their family, belongingness will be natural part of their life. Then teaching will be natural with students at the core. Students will also be more interactive and receptive. Unfortunately, it is missing in majority cases, so they focus on few students to whom teachers think good in studies or grades are better. teachers need to change their mindset. Will discuss about "Ancient Gurukul System" which is critically needed again.

- Most important point is "Art of encouraging questions". Teacher should not suppress the questions raised by students rather encourage and appreciate them. It makes them more creative, innovative, improves learning ability, builds confidence. Suppressing them gives an idea about themselves that they are not good in the eyes of teacher, asking questions is stupidity, feels isolated, feels like no space for creativity, innovation, conceptual and logical study.

My experience says, questions not only clear the doubts of students, but many times adds knowledge even for teachers. Let them develop a habit of theoretical, reasoning and logical ability which is essential for growth than "Rattafication". Even if they get little less marks, appreciate them for the right method of study and guide them so that in future they will improve in terms of grade as well.

> *"The beautiful thing about learning is that no one can take it from you."*

> ***Enjoy what you do so that everything else is worth it...***
>
> ***"Success is no accident. It is hard work, perseverance, learning, studying, sacrifice and most of all, love of what you are doing."***
>
> ***-Pele***

- The objective of any school or teachers shouldn't just be finishing the syllabus, but to work for overall development of a child. Plan in such a way that every week at least for 1 hour, teachers should interact with students about economy, politics, social issues, psychology, philosophy, unsung heroes, entertainment, health, food habits, spirituality, technological advancements. It will also help them to choose a right career path based on their interest and passion.

- Sports, Yoga, Pranayama, Meditation is equally important as curriculum. So, focus on both equally, one is complementary to other so one will enhance the value of the other and the overall performance will improve.

- Let them put in the activity/event/ project which they fear the most. If some student has stage fear, motivate them, let them know that you are with them mentally even if the performance is not up to the mark, it's OKAY. It will help them to overcome their fear.

"You Learn More From Failure Than From Success. Don't Let It Stop You. Failure Builds Character."

- *Disaster Management:* Emergency situations come up in life without advance intimation. Managing emergency situations require training to act under adverse conditions without going into the state of panic. School needs to train and prepare mind to handle adverse situations effectively without panicking. Let them take part in adventurous

26

activities with proper care and under expert supervision, it will develop a strong mind, will prepare them for future challenges as well as emergency situations.

Summary for teachers:

1. Belongingness
2. Leadership
3. Open minded
4. Believes in listening and not just lecturing
5. Encourage questioning without discouraging
6. Bringing out various qualities, dimensions of every child
7. Accepting students as they are and focus on their development
8. Creating a healthy competition, not being biased
9. Sharing and caring
10. Passionate about teaching

ANCIENT GURUKUL SYSTEM

India was once called "Sone ki Chidiya" (The Golden bird). During British colonization, Lord Macauley realized that, to rule India for a longer duration and to exploit it economic riches, its ancient education systems needs to be attacked, he successfully did that and brought their own system.

What is a Gurukul System?

It was a residential schooling system whose origin dates to around 5000 BC in the Indian subcontinents. It was more prevalent during the Vedic age, when students were taught various subjects and about how to live as cultured and disciplined being. Gurukul was mainly the home of teacher or Acharya and was the center of learning where pupils resided till their education completes. All were considered equally at the Gurukul and guru (teacher) as well as shishya (student) resided in the same house or lived near to each other. This relationship between guru and shishya was so sacred that no fee was taken from the students. However, the student had to offer a Gurudakshina which was a token of respect paid to the teacher. It was mainly in the form of money or a special task that the student had to perform for the teacher.

The importance of the Gurukul system in present times: -

The focus of Gurukuls was significantly on imparting learning to the students in a natural surrounding where the shishyas lived with each other with brotherhood, humanity, love, and discipline. The essential teachings were in subjects like language, science, mathematics through group discussions, self-learning etc. Not only this, but the focus was also given on arts, sports, crafts, singing that developed their intelligence and critical thinking. Activities such as yoga, meditation, mantra chanting etc., generated positivity and peace of mind and made them fit. It was also mandatory to do daily chores on their own with a motive to impart practical skills in them. All these helped in the personality development and increased their confidence, sense of discipline, intellect and mindfulness which is necessary even today to face the world that lay ahead.

Flaws in the present education system: -

Unfortunately, this ages old concept had disappeared, and the modern system of education brought into India in the year 1835 by Lord Macauley. This new system was all about unhealthy competition. There was a total absence of personality development that includes mind management, intellect, ego, memory and self (soul), creation of moral conscience and ethical training. One of the biggest drawbacks about this education was that it glorifies money oriented nature rather than an institutional concept that should impart holistic learning to the students. It just ignores or gives very little time for physical activity and the development of other skill sets (Practical Knowledge) that can assist a student to become a better human being.

Do we need a Gurukul system back in India?

Many people may consider the gurukul system to be quite old technique and not a scientific concept. However, the modern-day educationalist has taken a backward look and realized that there are many teaching approaches from the Gurukul system that can be inculcated in the present-day educational system. Here is a list to it that will also help us realize why the gurukul system in important.

- **Modern infrastructure –**

Robust learning of the students can only take place when focus is given on practical knowledge. But alas our present-day education just believes in bookish knowledge and cramming which is not enough. The Gurukul system focused on applied knowledge that prepared the students in all fields of life. In present times it can be done by creating a perfect combination of academics and extracurricular activities along with teaching in the area of mindfulness and spiritual awareness to make the students better individuals.

- **Holistic education –**

The present-day education mainly focuses on a rank-based system which is driven by animosity towards their peers. More fuel is added by the overambitious parents who judge the knowledge of students only by academic performance. The application of the Gurukul system instead can work on a value-based system where focus can be given on the uniqueness of child so that they can excel in their area of interest. This will also build a good character which is far away from fierce competition and increased stress levels that usually leads to depression.

- **The relation between teacher and student –**

The need of time is to ensure that teachers and students share a friendly relation and respect. This is as when the children feel secure and have trust in the teachers then they are most likely to emulate the same. This was present in the Gurukul system which can be inculcated today through use of activities, training workshops to bond with the students.

- **Personality Development –**

In Vedic education, a personality was developed through self-realization and self-respect. The end goal was building self-awareness, i.e., knowing oneself intimately. Good judgement had to be developed through practice. Daily tasks emphasizing on physical, mental, and emotional development. Students built their personalities in a multi-dimensional manner.

- **Character Formation –**

Ancient Indians did not believe that intellect alone was important, instead of that morality was considered the highest goal. Learning separated from morality was considered useless. Vedic education helped to form character by encouraging a simple life. Students were Brahmachari (celibate) till they were learning. Their live according to a strict schedule. Pleasures, comforts and luxuries were considered unnecessary. Plain food, good behavior and high ideals were encouraged. The gurus did not only teach the students but watched over their moral behavior as well.

- **Performance of Civic and Social Duties –**

The students' responsibility to society was made clear. In the gurukul, they all lived as equals, and participated in all works. Their daily tasks involved cleaning and keeping their residence in livable conditions. Their duty to the world outside their walls was also of great importance. They were made aware of the importance of being good spouses and parents. Their wealth was not to be used for their own wants, but for the good of society.

They were also taught to honor the codes of whatever professions they may choose in future.

- **Practical Education –**

Vedic education was not based solely on learning out of books. Hands on training in professions that interested the students was encouraged. They were taught the dignity of manual labor and the value of having a vocational training. Vocations included weaving, pottery and several other arts and professions.

- **Preservation and Spread of Culture –**

A large part of the Vedas is dedicated to traditions, cultures and rituals. Preservation of the literary and cultural traditions was necessary. Education was considered as the means to pass traditions to the next generation. Hence, the students were taught that they owed three debts — to the gods, to the past gurus, and to their ancestors. The students learned to serve the gods, which paid the first debt. The second was paid by learning the teachings of past intellectuals. The third debt to the ancestors was paid by raising children and educating them. Thus, all the traditions were preserved and passed on.

- **Achieving Enlightenment –**

While education was used to made students productive members of society, it had a spiritual element in it. Prayers and rituals were performed both daily and at important milestones such as birth, marriage, and death. This was done to teach each student the importance of the non-physical world. The aim was to lay an equal emphasis on body and soul.

- **Learning Process –**

Eligibility and Admission

Eligibility was not based on gender in Vedic times. Men and women alike studied the Vedas. There are records of several scholarly women and even women sages (Rishikas). There is some evidence that the Shudra caste (untouchables) was not allowed to study. While teachers were usually of the Brahmin caste, students could be Brahmin, Kshatriya or, Vaishya or Shudra.

Students were eligible once they underwent the upanayana or sacred thread ceremony. The child underwent this ceremony between the ages of 8 to 12. Studies usually went on for 12 years.

- **Curriculum –**

The Vedas — There are four Vedas — The Rigveda, the Yajurveda, the Samaveda and the Atharvaveda. These are classified as Samhitas, or mantras and benedictions.

The Aranyakas and Brahmanas — The Aranyakas are the text on rituals, ceremonies and sacrifices. The Brahmanas comment on those rituals.

Upanishads — These texts discuss meditation, philosophy and the spiritual world.

Vedangas — These consist of six areas of study: Phonetics, ritualistic knowledge, grammar, exegetics (the science of interpretation), metrics and astronomy.

- **Methods of Teaching –**

Memorization — Learning the sacred texts by heart is an essential step in studying the Vedas. Repetition and recitation by the teacher and students were important.

Introspection — This has three steps. The first is Shraavana, which means listening to texts recited by the teacher. This is how the student absorbs the teacher's knowledge. The second is Manana, which involves deliberation and reflection. The student what has been taught and what they can learn from it. The third step is Nididhyasana, or meditation. This is the step through which truth is realized and attained.

Critical Analysis — The students are taught to think critically and come to their own conclusions. Students may even disagree with their teachers and bring them around to their way of thinking.

Hands-on Learning — Learning by doing was encouraged, especially as many students went into trades later. In areas such as medicine, observation and practice were necessary.

Seminars — Debates and discussions were held often. Students could discuss topics of interest and put their views forward.

- **Higher Studies –**

While some students went to their trades or professions, many continued to learn. Institutions known as Parishads were places of higher learning. Advanced students gathered there to learn through discussion and discourse. Three Brahmins conducted these sessions. Eventually that increased to 21 Brahmins learned in theology and philosophy. In today's world, they would be considered equal to colleges.

Scholars would continue learning through their life by attending Sammelans (gatherings). These were discussions and competitions in which some of the most learned people in the country participated. They were often presided over by kings, who invited the scholars.

- **Modern Efforts for Vedic Education –**

Private Efforts

People around India have taken on the effort to bring back the philosophies of Vedic education. Privately funded gurukuls have sprung up around the country. They are often run by religious and spiritual trusts. They take in students on a residential basis. Spirituality and traditional values are of importance in these institutes. The accommodation and food are usually simple and basic, as they would be in Vedic times. Parents often pick these for children stressed by the burden of the modern educational system.

Final words: -

Overall, the idea of inculcating a Gurukul system in Indian education system is to assist the children to understand the concept of a balanced life. This very ideology of balance should be taught to the kids from a young age so that they make informed decisions about work, food, exercise and the way they wish to live their life.

Basically, we need an education system which cover ancient-modern approach. We as a parent should convince government to open and allow to open these schools in large scale.

PHYSICAL/SEXUAL ATTRACTION (LUST)

> *"In love the other is important; in lust you are important"*
>
> **— Osho**

It is natural to feel attracted towards oppositely sex especially after puberty. Hormonal changes and change in physical appearance lead to attraction. But if the boundary of this attraction is crossed then it turns out be a disastrous for a youngster. Swami Vivekanand said, "Anything in excess is poison". Let's see how it affects mind and distracts from goal.

A weak mind watching porn sites, when the adolescents doesn't get love at home, they try to find out the same outside. These are some of the reasons of strongly getting attracted physically or sexually and they call it as love. Is it love?? No, it is lust. They are attracted towards the various organs of opposite partner which gives them the sensation of arousal. They seem to show that they have bonded with each other emotionally and a bonding within, but factually, everything is superficial, and it is just an urge to satisfy physical needs and see partner as an object of pleasure.

"The whole sexual attraction thing, people are judging for partnership."

Problems starts on mental level, mind gets completely soaked and blocked in thinking of partner, the focus on studies, goals goes out of the track, bunking school, lying to parents, finding ways to meet by any means and in some cases even intercourse as they are quite aware about the availability of contraceptive pills, forgetting the worst kind of side effects in near future. Since the attraction is purely physical. One of the traits of the mind is that, it's always looks for new things/objects, after some time as it gets bored with the same person/object for some duration. So, they break away, and both get mentally and emotionally disturbed. They have already wasted lot of time, which has affected their studies. Sometimes, this lead to suicidal tendencies and in some cases cause actual suicide. The emotions overpowers a person with such experience, so much that they forget about the parents who are loving unconditionally and putting all the efforts to make them successful and how their life will become miserable after worst kind of departure.

Writing more about suicidal tendency and how to overcome it in coming chapter.

My request to all youngsters is to keep a strong mind and realize that time never roles back, the schooling age won't come back so if you lose track of studies, it will lead you to difficult life in future. On the other hand, what you are looking too early in life about sex and sexual life, you are eventually going to get for whole life after your marriage so why to waste our precious time on something which we are going to get in future easily and lose sight on something important like becoming whatever your passion is, through education.

> **"Life and Time is precious, so don't waste it on things which you can get easily."**

SPIRITUALITY: IMPORTANT DIMENSION OF LIFE

> **The goal of Spirituality is to bring such happiness, which nobody can take away from you**
>
> **- Sri Sri Ravi Shankar**

Introduction to Spirituality

In his book "Save Your Brain," Dr. Paul Nussbaum – an eminent Neuropsychologist, says our Brain demands stimulation, but it can function best when it is in rhythm and symmetry. Our hectic pace can cause stress, chaos and loss of brain efficiency, so from time to time our brains need to slow down and re-energize. Dr. Nussbaum refers to this phase as "Spirituality."

Many of us have explored Spirituality in our own ways. Although this quest is very personal (i.e., we all have our own personal definition of Spirituality), it is collective in spirit. This is because Spirituality in people's minds is synonymous of a search for meaning, for purpose and direction in life.

People get attracted to Spirituality and embark on their spiritual journeys for different reasons. Generically, there are a few main reasons for this.

Curiosity about the spiritual dimension: This includes seeking answers to the more profound questions in life such as – what is the purpose of life, from where did I come from and where do we will go after death?

When facing a problem in life: Insurmountable problems in life are often a catalyst for people to search for answers to their problems beyond the purview of modern science. This includes approaching an astrologer, a psychic or a spiritual Guru/leader.

Interested in spiritual healing: The ability to heal by channelizing subtle energies is an art that has been pursued for millennia.

Interested in personality improvement: Wanting to be a better person can lead one to Spirituality and a more spiritual way of life.

Wanting to grow spiritually: Some of us have an innate need to grow spiritually and do not need a catalyst to push us towards Spirituality.

Spirituality helps in overcoming:

Definition of Spirituality

> *Worrying doesn't make any difference, but working does; and spirituality gives one the strength to work: Sri Sri Ravi Shankar*

In Sanskrit, Spirituality is known as Adhyātma. It is derived from two words Adhi and Ātman (Ātmanahā). Adhi means pertaining to the topic and Ātmā means the Soul. The Soul is the God principle within each of us and is our true nature. It is the main constituent of the subtle body, which is a fractional part of the Supreme God Principle. It's traits are Absolute Truth (Sat), Absolute Consciousness (Chit) and Bliss (Ānand). The Soul is unaffected by the ups and downs (and the happiness and unhappiness) one experiences in life as it is perpetually in a blissful state.

Spirituality does not mean going away from life, spirituality means becoming alive in the fullest possible way so you are not just alive on the surface, you are alive to the core : Jaggi Vasudev

What are human beings made of? (Body, Mind, Intellect, Soul or something else).

Our natural state is to be blissful (which is the nature of the Soul within us) and we all inherently yearn to be in this state. This is also the reason why we all search for happiness in life and run after numerous things that we think will make us happy. However, as we all know with the stresses and tensions of modern-day living, 'happiness' is elusive and fleeting.

Spirituality, thus, deals with understanding the nature of the Soul and one's journey back to identifying the Soul and experiencing it as one's true nature. Spirituality is the expansive science about how to be blissful.

The scope of the science of Spirituality is vast and also includes answers to profound questions such as, 'who am I', 'where did I come from', 'what is the purpose of life', 'where will I go after death', etc.

In Sanskrit, Spirituality or Spiritual science it is called "Paravidya" (Supreme science), while all other Sciences are called "Aparāvidyā" meaning inferior Science. By 'science', we mean modern science. Rationalists and most people think that Science and Spirituality are two separate disciplines. However, Spirituality is the knowledge about infinity, that is, knowledge of all subjects. It covers the whole physical world and the subtle unseen world, all the physical and spiritual regions, all physical and subtle frequencies, energies and vibrations, all positive and negative entities and all living beings and non-living beings in the whole Universe. Spirituality contains all the knowledge and memory of the past, present and future, from the beginning to the end of the Universe.

Difference between Spirituality and religion

For many people, religion provides them their first lessons about spiritual matters and things that are beyond the physical world. However, religions often tend to be sectarian in nature. A 'sect' is a group of people who usually think that their "Path to God" is the best and the preferable one (if not the only one).

However, one of the fundamental principles of Spirituality is that there are as many paths to God as there are people. Just as a doctor does not advise the same medicine for different ailments which different people may have, similarly the same type of spiritual practice does not necessarily benefit everyone. When spiritual practice is tailor-made as per the temperament and needs of an individual, it leads to faster spiritual progress.

God is expansive, and to experience Him, we too must become expansive in our spiritual outlook. A myopic or ethnocentric outlook about religion or Spirituality often stifles spiritual growth, thus leading to stagnation.

Why is Spirituality vital to us?

Regardless of who we are and where we come from – our desire to experience happiness in our lives drives all our worldly pursuits. This need is common to all of us. Regardless of cultural background, religion, gender, social or financial status, etc. However, through spiritual research, we have found that on average people experience happiness only 30% of the time.

One of the main reasons we experience sadness is due to problems in life. Everyone knows about the physical and psychological causes of problems in life. However, what many of us do not know is that problems that are physical or psychological in nature and could have a spiritual root cause. This means that even though a problem is primarily due to spiritual reasons, it can manifest as a physical or psychological problem.

The main spiritual problems destiny (karma), problems due to departed ancestors and distress due to negative energies.

Breakdown of the root cause of difficulties in a person's life

Through spiritual research, we have found that over 50% of the problems that a person faces in life are due to spiritual reasons. All major events in life like marriage, good and bad relationships, serious accidents and major illnesses are mostly because one's destiny.

Now this is important – The solution for any problem needs to be provided at that corresponding level.

The solution for a problem needs to be at that corresponding level.

When the problem of a patient has a spiritual root cause, it is best to provide spiritual help or employ a spiritual solution to problem. Spiritual measures such as practicing Spirituality provide relief to the physical and psychological problems as well and this is especially so if the root cause of the problem is spiritual in nature.

Spirituality and the purpose of life

At some point of time in our lives some of us begin to wonder – Is this it?

Is this all there is in life – for example – getting a good education, earning money, getting a loan, purchasing a car, getting an even bigger loan, purchasing a house, purchasing a bigger house, achieving success and recognition in some field, raising a family and then ultimately die? Some of us may begin to wonder whether life has any higher purpose or not.

For those of us who have gone through this stage of introspection, it is like something has shifted deep within us. For some of us, such feelings have propelled us to embark on our own spiritual journeys.

According to the science of Spirituality, there are only 2 reasons for being born:

- The fundamental purpose of life is to complete one's destiny or karma that one is born with.

- The secondary and more important purpose of life is to grow spiritually.

Practicing Spirituality as per universal principles helps with both these purposes. It helps to burn adverse destiny that causes us unhappiness and it also helps us to grow spiritually.

Spirituality is a pragmatic science

Many of us have read books on Spirituality and spiritual concepts. However, in mere theory (even if it is correct) apart from providing direction to an individual, unless it is put into practice can never be experienced. It remains as just intellectual spiritual concepts to a person. Only when one puts that knowledge into practice, does one get spiritual experiences or the experience of Spirituality. Spiritual practice truly helps a person understand the importance of Spirituality. Therefore, it is said that in a person's spiritual journey, theoretical knowledge of Spirituality has only 2% importance, while 98% importance is for practicing.

If a person just reads about Spirituality and does not practice it, he will never understand or experience its importance. As a result, sooner or later he may stop having any interest in it. In fact, he may also end up doubting its usefulness in life.

Summary: Why Spirituality: -

1. A means to arrive at peace for ourselves and others.

2. Spirituality is a feeling or an insight. When peace comes over you by experiencing (seeing or hearing) something that makes you feel good.

3. Looking at the moon, stars, sun and universe spread out to infinity and feeling at peace.

4. Acknowledge the creation of all we see and realize it all is created by a force or matter from a creator.

5. Doing something good for others.

6. Using your mind and not only your eyes.

7. Loving and caring for all people and be thankful there is a higher power watching over all of us.

8. A belief in something greater than yourself. Being good and positive and avoiding negative thoughts.

9. God is with us everywhere.

10. It is a sense of inner peace and contentment of oneself. A feeling of belonging and being tranquil.

11. How will learning about spirituality help them to live on this Earth?

12. It promotes peace.

13. They will convene with others and avoid hostility.

14. Its communication. Let's communicate!

15. Showing a trust to understand the idea of creation and share with all.

16. Pass on good.

17. They will understand what they see. Role models.

18. We are all in this together and we should be caring and loving toward everyone.

19. They will learn to care for others.

20. God guides us and you to do what we should do!

21. It will provide a sense of belonging and avoid loneliness.

MEDITATION

Meditation is simply doing nothing during meditation process.

Meditation is a simple way of freeing your mind, forgetting about daily anxieties and focusing on mental relaxation. Going into a meditative state involves learning to become a passive observer of one's thoughts. It does not mean suppressing them or attempting to force them to disappear.

Meditation is the process of continuous focus on one object for a prolonged period. It is a gentle, subtle method which does not require any force or pressure on the mind. The result you gain out of the practice is increased concentration and focus.

Just like developing any other skill, meditation requires regularity of practice. There are common misconceptions that meditation is something difficult, which requires years of practice to achieve any kind of result. This is simply untrue. People often report feeling the benefits of meditation immediately after their first session. You can begin today and experience it yourself with just a few steps.

Benefits of Meditation:

Meditation do magic by changing the actual brain. MRI Brain images show that regular meditators have more activity in the left prefrontal cortex, an area of the brain associated with feelings of joy and equanimity. Meditation also increases the thickness of the cerebral cortex and encourages more connections between brain cells—all of which increases mental sharpness and memory ability.

How many times have you felt that 24 hours are not enough in a day? Whether you're a student or a professional, you are trapped in this fast-moving world, where it is increasingly more difficult to find time for oneself.

Usually, when we take a break from our busy schedules, we spend time on our mobile phones or laptops. It is harmful not only for the eyes but also for the mind. The mind is like a pendulum. It keeps swinging from one extremity to another. What we require is centeredness. To regulate the mind and give it some rest, the best medicine you can give it is meditation.

Yes, that's right!

Meditation acts like a battery-recharger. Just 10 minutes of meditation will make you feel calm and refreshed and better able to tackle the rest of your workload.

So how does meditation help us to maximize the 24 hours of the day? Here we go:

- **Reduces stress and brings peace:**

Most people understand that meditation reduces stress and promotes peace of mind. As you allow your mind to settle on one continuous thought, instead of being pulled in all directions, your stress level reduces. Other health problems like high blood pressure, irregular or high heartbeat, high pulse rate, abnormal breathing patterns, and anxiety also are regulated.

- **Helps in concentration:**

Meditation is a great aid for regulating your mind. The mind's tendency is to think a lot and to be easily pulled in different directions depending on our personal likes and dislikes. When you pay attention to every unnecessary thought, you are drawn away from what is truly important. Practicing meditation helps you to gently ignore what is unnecessary and focus more on what is important. This gives you greater clarity and makes you faster and more capable of anything that you do.

- **Helps you sleep better:**

If you have ever laid your head on a pillow and then struggled for hours to sleep because of thoughts racing through your mind, then meditation is ideal for you! We are often stuck in limbo, worrying about the past and the future which interferes with our sleep at night. If you practice meditation on a regular basis, you will gradually begin to cherish the present moment. Worries of the day and the future will not trouble you, allowing you to sleep soundly. When you wake up the next morning, you'll feel lighter and fresher. Maintaining a balanced sleep cycle can help to eliminate many health problems.

- **Makes you emotionally stronger:**

Wondering how? During the meditation process, where we are constantly focusing our attention on one thing, we learn to let go of unnecessary thoughts. Meditation is a process of spending time with yourself and is a journey of self-discovery. By understanding ourselves, we can build our emotional resilience and tap into our inner intuition. Daily struggles and irritations will no longer impact you, as you remain centered in yourself and the present moment.

- **Keeps you active throughout the day:**

One who is committed to balancing their mental energies is also a lot more energized. The positivity that you develop in your mind will give you the zest and enthusiasm to maximize your productivity throughout the day. When you feel calmer and happier, your relationships with people around you grow stronger.

When we meditate, we inject far-reaching and long-lasting benefits into our lives: We lower our stress levels, we get to know our pain, we connect better, we improve our focus, and we're kinder to ourselves. Let us walk you through the basics in our new mindful guide on how to meditate.

INTELLECT AND MEMORY

> **The intellect of the wise is like glass; it admits the light of heaven and reflects it.**
>
> **Augustus Hare**

How to boost brain power at any age: -

A strong memory depends on the health and vitality of your brain. Whether you're a student studying for final exams, a working professional interested in doing all you can to stay mentally sharp, or a senior looking to preserve and enhance your grey matter as you age, there's lots you can do to improve your memory and mental performance.

Many says, you can't teach an old dog new tricks, but when it comes to the brain, scientists have discovered that this adage simply isn't true. The human brain has an astonishing ability to adapt and change—even into old age. This ability is known as neuroplasticity. With the right stimulation, your brain can form new neural pathways, alter existing connections, and adapt and react in ever-changing ways.

The brain's incredible ability to reshape itself holds true when it comes to learning and memory. You can harness the natural power of neuroplasticity to increase your cognitive abilities, enhance your ability to learn new information, and improve your memory at any age.

These 9 Tips Can Show You How

Tip 1: Give your brain a workout

By the time you've reached adulthood, your brain has developed millions of neural pathways that help you process and recall information quickly, solve familiar problems, and execute habitual tasks with a minimum of mental effort. But if you always stick to these well-worn paths, you aren't giving your brain the stimulation it needs to keep growing and developing. You must shake things up from time to time!

Memory, like muscular strength, requires you to "use it or lose it." The more you work out your brain, the better you'll be able to process and remember information. But not all activities are equal. The best brain exercises break your routine and challenge you to use and develop new brain pathways.

Four key elements of a good brain-boosting activity

It teaches you something new - No matter how intellectually demanding the activity, if it's something you're already good at, it's not a good brain exercise. The activity needs to be something that's unfamiliar and out of your comfort zone. To strengthen the brain, you need to keep learning and developing new skills.

It's challenging - The best brain-boosting activities demand your full and close attention. It's not enough that you found the activity challenging at one point. It must still be something that requires mental effort. For example, learning to play a challenging new piece of music counts. Playing a difficult piece, you've already memorized does not.

It's a skill you can build on - Look for activities that allow you to start at an easy level and work your way up as your skills improve —always pushing the envelope so you continue to stretch your capabilities. When a previously difficult level starts to feel comfortable, that means it's time to tackle the next level of performance.

It's rewarding - Rewards support the brain's learning process. The more interested and engaged you are in the activity, the more likely you'll continue doing it and the greater the benefits you'll experience. So, choose activities that, while challenging, are still enjoyable and satisfying.

Closeup of a guitar being played. Think of something new you've always wanted to try, like learning how to play the guitar, make pottery, juggle, play chess, speak French, dance the tango, or master your golf swing. Any of these activities can help you improve your memory, so until it keeps you challenged and engaged.

What about brain-training programs?

There are countless brain-training apps and online programs that promise to boost memory, problem-solving skills, attention, and even IQ with daily practice. But do they really work? Increasingly, the evidence says no. While these brain-training programs may lead to short-term improvements in whatever task or specific game you've been practicing, they don't appear to strengthen or improve overall intelligence, memory, or other cognitive abilities.

Tip 2: Don't skip the physical exercise

While mental exercise is important for brain health, that doesn't mean you never need to break a sweat. Physical exercise helps your brain stay sharp. It increases oxygen to your brain and reduces the risk for disorders that lead to memory loss, such as diabetes and cardiovascular disease. Exercise also enhances the effects of helpful brain chemicals and reduces stress hormones. Perhaps most importantly, exercise plays an important role in neuroplasticity by boosting growth factors and stimulating new neuronal connections.

Brain-boosting exercise tips

Aerobic exercise is particularly good for the brain, so choose activities that keep your blood pumping. In general, anything that is good for your heart is great for your brain.

Does it take you long time to clear out the sleep fog when you wake up? If so, you may find that exercising in the morning before you start your day makes a big difference. In addition to clearing out the cobwebs, it also primes you for learning throughout the day.

Physical activities that require hand-eye coordination or complex motor skills are particularly beneficial for brain building.

Exercise breaks can help you get past mental fatigue and afternoon slumps. Even a short walk or a few jumping jacks can be enough to reboot your brain.

Tip 3: Get your Zest

There is a big difference between the amount of sleep you can get by on and the amount you need to function at your best. The truth is that over 95% of adults need between 7.5 to 9 hours of sleep every night in order to avoid sleep deprivation. Even skimping on a few hours makes a difference! Memory, creativity, problem-solving abilities, and critical thinking skills are all compromised.

But sleep is critical to learning and memory in an even more fundamental way. Research shows that sleep is necessary for memory consolidation, with the key memory-enhancing activity occurring during the deepest stages of sleep.

Get on a regular sleep schedule. Go to bed at the same time every night and get up at the same time each morning. Try not to break your routine, even on weekends and holidays.

Avoid all screens for at least an hour before bed. The blue light emitted by TVs, tablets, phones, and computers trigger wakefulness and suppress hormones such as melatonin that make you sleepy.

Cut back on caffeine. Caffeine affects people differently. Some people are highly sensitive, and even morning coffee may interfere with sleep at night. Try reducing your intake or cutting it out entirely if you suspect it's keeping you up.

Tip 4: Make time for friends

When you think of ways to improve memory, do you think of "serious" activities such as wrestling with crossword puzzle or mastering chess strategy, or is it more lighthearted pastimes—hanging out with friends or enjoying a funny movie—that come to mind? If you're like most of us, it's probably the former. But countless studies show that a life full of friends and fun comes with cognitive benefits.

Healthy relationships: the ultimate brain booster

Humans are highly social animals. We're not meant to survive, let alone thrive, in isolation. Relationships stimulate our brains—in fact, interacting with others may provide the best kind of brain exercise.

Research shows that having meaningful friendships and a strong support system are vital not only to emotional health, but also to brain health. In one recent study from the Harvard School of Public Health, for example, researchers found that people with the most active social lives had the slowest rate of memory decline.

There are many ways to start taking advantage of the brain and memory-boosting benefits of socializing. Volunteer, join a club, make it a point to see friends more often, or reach out over the phone. And if a human isn't handy, don't overlook the value of a pet—especially the highly-social dog.

Tip 5: Keep stress in check

Stress is one of the brain's worst enemies. Over time, chronic stress destroys brain cells and damages the hippocampus, the region of the brain involved in the formation of new memories and the retrieval of old ones. Studies have also linked stress to memory loss.

Tips for managing stress

- Set realistic expectations (and be willing to say no!)
- Take breaks throughout the day
- Express your feelings instead of piling them up
- Set a healthy balance between work and leisure time
- Focus on one task at a time, rather than trying to multi-task

The stressbusting, memory-boosting benefits of meditation

The scientific evidence on the mental health benefits of meditation continues to pile up. Studies show that meditation helps improve many different types of conditions, including depression, anxiety, chronic pain, diabetes, and high blood pressure. Meditation also can improve focus, concentration, creativity, memory, and learning and reasoning skills.

Tip 6: Have a laugh

You've heard that laughter is the best medicine, and that holds true for the brain and the memory, as well as the body. Unlike emotional responses, which are limited to specific areas of the brain, laughter engages multiple regions across the whole brain.

Furthermore, listening to jokes and working out punch lines activates areas of the brain vital to learning and creativity. As psychologist Daniel Goleman notes in his book Emotional Intelligence, "laughter seems to help people think more broadly and associate more freely."

Looking for ways to bring more laughter in your life? Start with these basics:

Laugh at yourself - Share your embarrassing moments. The best way to take ourselves less seriously is to talk about the times when we took ourselves too seriously.

When you hear laughter, move toward it. Most of the time, people are very happy to share something funny because it gives them an opportunity to laugh again and feed off the humor you find in it. When you hear laughter, seek it out and try to join in.

Spend time with fun, playful people - These are people who laugh easily—both at themselves and at life's absurdities—and who routinely find the humor in everyday events. Their playful point of view and laughter are contagious.

Surround yourself with reminders to lighten up - Keep a toy on your desk or in your car. Put up a funny poster in your office. Choose a computer screensaver that makes you laugh. Frame photos of you and your loved ones having fun.

Pay attention to children and emulate them. They are the experts on playing, taking life lightly, and laughing.

Tip 7: Eat a brain-boosting diet

Just as the body needs fuel, so does the brain. You probably already know that a diet based on fruits, vegetables, whole grains, "healthy" fats (such as olive oil, nuts, etc.) and lean protein will provide lots of health benefits, but such a diet can also improve memory. For brain health, though, it's not just what you eat—it's also what you do not eat. The following nutritional tips will help boost your brainpower and reduce your risk of dementia:

Get your omega-3s - Research shows that omega-3 fatty acids are particularly beneficial for brain health. The sources of omega-3s such as seaweed, walnuts, ground flaxseed, flaxseed oil, winter squash, kidney and pinto beans, spinach, broccoli, pumpkin seeds, and soybeans.

Limit calories and saturated fat - Research shows that diets high in saturated fat (from sources such as red meat, whole milk, butter, cheese, cream, and ice cream) increase your risk of dementia and impair concentration and memory.

Eat more fruit and vegetables - Produce is packed with antioxidants, substances that protect your brain cells from damage. Colorful fruits and vegetables are particularly good antioxidant "superfood" sources.

Drink green tea - Green tea contains polyphenols, powerful antioxidants that protect against free radicals that can damage brain cells. Among many other benefits, regular consumption of green tea may enhance memory and mental alertness and slow brain aging.

Tip 8: Identify and treat health problems

Do you feel that your memory has taken an unexplainable dip? If so, there may be a health or lifestyle problem to blame.

It's not just dementia or Alzheimer's disease that causes memory loss. There are many diseases, mental health disorders, and medications that can interfere with memory:

Heart disease and its risk factors - Cardiovascular disease and its risk factors, including high cholesterol and high blood pressure, have been linked to mild cognitive impairment.

Diabetes - Studies show that people with diabetes experience far greater cognitive decline than those who don't suffer from the disease.

Hormone imbalance - Women going through menopause often experience memory problems when their estrogen dips. In men, low testosterone can cause issues. Thyroid imbalances can also cause forgetfulness, sluggish thinking, or confusion.

Medications - Many prescription and over-the-counter medications can get in the way of memory and clear thinking. Common culprits include cold and allergy medications, sleep aids, and antidepressants. Talk to your doctor or pharmacist about possible side effects.

Is it depression?

Emotional difficulties can take just as heavy a toll on the brain as physical problems. In fact, mental sluggishness, difficulty concentrating, and forgetfulness are common symptoms of depression. The memory issues can be particularly bad in older people who are depressed-so much so that it is sometimes mistaken for dementia. The good news is that when the depression is treated, memory should return to normal.

Tip 9: Take practical steps to support learning and memory

Pay attention - You can't remember something if you never learned it, and you can't learn something—that is, encode it into your brain—if you don't pay enough attention to it. It takes about eight seconds of intense focus to process a piece of information into your memory. If you're easily distracted, pick a quiet place where you won't be interrupted.

Involve as many senses as possible - Try to relate information to colors, textures, smells, and tastes. The physical act of rewriting information can help imprint it onto your brain. Even if you're a visual learner, read out loud what you want to remember. If you can recite it rhythmically, even better.

Relate information to what you already know - Connect new data to information you already remember, whether it's new material that builds on previous knowledge, or something as simple as an address of someone who lives on a street where you already know someone.

For more complex material, focus on understanding basic ideas rather than memorizing isolated details. Practice explaining the ideas to someone else in your own words.

Rehearse information you've already learned - Review what you've learned the same day you learn it, and at intervals thereafter. This "spaced rehearsal" is more effective than cramming, especially for retaining what you've learned.

Use mnemonic (the initial "m" is silent) devices to make memorization easier - Mnemonics are clues of any kind that help us remember something, usually by helping us associate the information we want to remember with a visual image, a sentence, or a word.

6 Types Of Mnemonic Device

Visual image – Associate a visual image with a word or name to help you remember them better. Positive, pleasant images that are vivid, colorful, and three-dimensional will be easier to remember. Example: To remember the name Rosa Parks and what she's known for, picture a woman sitting on a park bench surrounded by roses, waiting as her bus pulls up.

Acrostic (or sentence) – Make up a sentence in which the first letter of each word is part of or represents the initial of what you want to remember. Example: The sentence "Every good boy does fine" to memorize the lines of the treble clef, representing the notes E, G, B, D, and F.

Acronym – An acronym is a word that is made up by taking the first letters of all the key words or ideas you need to remember and creating a new word out of them. Example: The word "HOMES" to remember the names of the Great Lakes: Huron, Ontario, Michigan, Erie, and Superior.

Rhymes and alliteration – Rhymes, alliteration (a repeating sound or syllable), and even jokes are memorable way to remember more mundane facts and figures. Example: The rhyme "Thirty days hath September, April, June, and November" to remember the months of the year with only 30 days in them.

Chunking – Chunking breaks a long list of numbers or other types of information into smaller, more manageable chunks. Example: Remembering a 10-digit phone number by breaking it down into three sets of numbers: 555-867-5309 (as opposed to 5558675309).

Method of loci – Imagine placing the items you want to remember along a route you know well, or in specific locations in a familiar room or building. Example: For a shopping list, imagine bananas in the entryway to your home, a puddle of milk in the middle of the sofa, eggs going up the stairs, and bread on your bed.

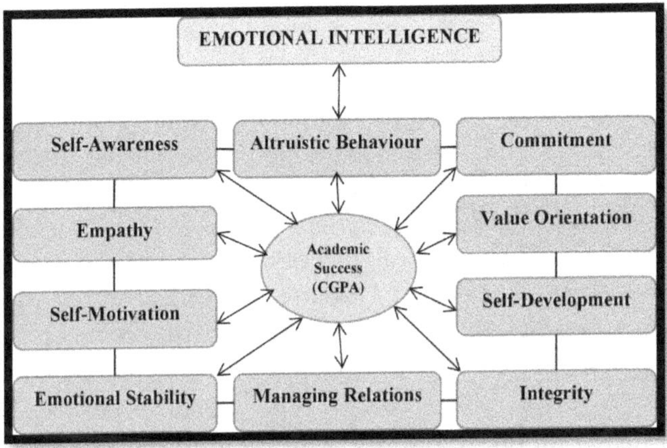

Memory is the faculty of the brain by which data or information is encoded, stored, and retrieved when needed. It is the retention of information over time for the purpose of influencing future action. If past events could not be remembered, it would be impossible for language, relationships, or personal identity to develop. Memory loss is usually described as forgetfulness or amnesia.

UNDERSTANDING EGO

Learning human ego is one of the most powerful ways through which you can learn more about yourself and gain a greater understanding of others.

Our ego is our perception of oneself and how we are perceived by the outside world. Everyone has an ego; it is a natural facet of our humanity. What we invest our egos into has major implications on the way that we act, what we believe, and how we respond to adversity such as criticism, insults, and failure. Ego means, you are either in superiority complex or inferiority complex than your natural state. You constantly compare yourself with others, you feel low if other is superior and vice-versa.

Like many things, the concept of ego often gets misrepresented. When referring to the "ego" people are often referring to someone's ego investment into a belief or set of beliefs, or they may say that someone has a "big" ego, which is a high belief in a person's self-worth typically combined with a personality trait such as arrogance or cockiness. These references may be like the definition of the ego, but they are not referring to what the ego is.

Understanding how and where to invest your ego will give you a better control over your emotions and judgment. Additionally, it will give you a lot of insight into how other people behave, and how their egos are invested. We will discuss the ego and how you can use your understanding of it to gain more control over yourself and ultimately a greater understanding of the world around you.

"Always remember, when you are on the path of success, be remain grounded and in failure, let your ego say nothing can destroy me."

EGO

Three little letters

That keeps us from

Saying things, we

Really like to say

Like

I love you

I miss you

I am sorry

Types of Ego: -

1. Pure ego

This is a state where traces of ego are seen in Saints of the highest order when they are not in complete communion with God. These Saints have just a mere awareness of one's existence. This trace ego is required for the sustenance of body functions.

Pure ego can be understood as having the following attitudes:

- Considering oneself to be distinct or separate from Brahman (God principle), that is harboring awareness of the self through duality.
- Having awareness of one's existence.
- Harboring the spiritual emotion (bhava) that 'I belong to others and all are mine'.

2. Impure ego

This type of ego is what most of us experience. Almost all of us identify with our physical body, or feelings and emotions and feel pride in our intellect. This is due to various impressions in the centers of the subtle body like temperamental characteristics, desires, likes and dislikes, etc.

Depending on thoughts and emotions, this ego can be either sāttvik (Sattva predominant), rājasik (Raja predominant) or tāmasik (Tama predominant).

1. Tamasik ego: The ego which is subtle basic Tama component predominant is called tamasik ego, e.g. believing only in one's own capability.
2. Rajasik ego: Subtle basic Raja component predominant ego is called rajasik ego, e.g. constantly striving for happiness.
3. Sattvik ego: Ego which is predominant in the subtle basic Sattva component is called sattvik ego, e.g. ego about sacrifice is sattvik in nature.

9 Signs You're Letting Your Ego Run Your Life
Ego-Selfie

Sigmund Freud, the father of psychoanalysis, studied a very complex set of theories about the human ego. He surmised the following basic precepts.

- Psychological problems are rooted in the unconscious mind.
- Psychological symptoms are the result of hidden (unconscious) thoughts.
- Most cases of psychological problems are directly attributable to issues during development (childhood) or repressed trauma.
- Treatment focuses on bringing the unresolved, subconscious conflict into consciousness; allowing the patient to deal with the problem.

In layman's term, the ego is responsible for mediating impulses and desires with responsible, socially acceptable actions. But those with excessive egos do not adequately balance their desires with action; instead, they act on what is most self-serving, instantaneous, and beneficial – otherwise known as immediate gratification.

> *"We must go beyond the constant clamor of ego, beyond the tools of logic and reason, to the still, calm place within us: the realm of the soul."*
>
> *– Deepak Chopra*

Here Are 9 Signs Your Ego Is In Control Of Your Life:

1. Too much is never enough

Greed can bring down an individual, a family… even a society. It means urge to achieve success, possess nice things and have some security. It isn't normal to have an insatiable desire to attain the most of something– money, cars, homes, power, etc. In fact, such behavior is included in the textbook definition of narcist behavior.

If you want to see what greed can do to an individual, type 'Bernie Madoff' or 'Charles Ponzi' on Google search. What insatiable greed can do to a society, type in 'Great Depression' or '2008 financial crises'. While these may be considered extreme examples by some, such events began with the gluttonous thoughts and actions of one person.

Takeaway: Attempt to rein in your impulses to always acquire a more, while showing gratitude about what you already have.

2. Disliking when people succeed

Could you remember when your friends did better in exam? What was your reaction? Were you happy for the person or envious of what they've attained?

People with large egos don't appreciate when someone achieves success; especially success that they feel was rightfully theirs.

Takeaway: Even if you don't want to congratulate someone, do it anyways. You'll feel better and likely find that more doors open for you.

3. Redirecting the attention back to you

Here's something interesting: attention seekers are likely to have inflated egos. That's not all that interesting. It makes perfect sense because everything is about them!

The need to always be the center of attention no matter what – in meetings, at parties, during conversations, etc.– is a telltale sign that the ego has become a little too big. Everyone should have the chance to be seen and heard.

Takeaway: Always remember, attention brings tension. Understand that attention-seeking behavior is counter-productive; it's also obnoxious, rude, and annoying. Even when you may not necessarily feel like it, give others the chance to be seen and heard.

4. Constantly comparing yourself

Here's the thing: no matter what you do; the skills you have; the talent you're born with; the look that you've got; the intelligence that you possess – you'll find someone, somewhere that is "more" talented, attractive, smarter, and successful.

Comparing yourself only succeeds at one thing – making you upset and potentially undermining any progress that you've achieved in the process. It's an absolute waste of time and energy. Being the best possible at what you're attempting to achieve is all that you should need.

Takeaway: Instead of likening yourself with others, focus on what you can control – your effort, progress, and persistence. You're a special, unique person, and you shouldn't require validation by comparing yourself with others.

5. Craving respect and recognition

The urge to feel appreciated is normal and healthy. We all want to experience our contributions are recognized and valued by others. Egotists take this need to another level by always needing to feel validated through excessive acts of respect and recognition.

You've likely seen this in the school or workplace at one time or another; maybe a classmate, co-worker or boss who incessantly sought recognition for virtually everything that they achieved from the time that they clocked in.

Takeaway: The only respect that you aspire should be self-respect. The fact that you've done a good job and gave your best effort is enough. People will recognize your efforts and contributions, while in turn giving you the respect and recognition that is due.

6. Always being defensive

The ego is something that will protect and defend itself from unpleasant feelings. For those with an excessive ego, they will pick up any subtle disagreement and turn it into an argument. They perceive any resistance to their thoughts and actions as "attacks".

Being defensive on a continuous basis can damage relationships, career and personal growth, and make them more critical – of themselves and others. It's simply a bad personality trait to have.

Takeaway: Make attempts to listen actively, and must accept counter argument and constructive criticism. People who resists a thought or idea are often not trying to express contempt to your stand, so don't take it personally.

7. Rarely (if ever) helping others

People who have ego problems are very individualistic, if a situation does not pertain to them then it's not worth their time or effort. We see this often in societies defined by class and status. The result has been the degradation of the social contract, the indifference to suffering, and the increased emphasis on materialism.

Do something positive for those who are less fortunate, by giving donations or volunteer services. Don't buy the notion of, "accumulation of wealth and possessions will raise your class status".

Takeaway: Do something to help others instead of focusing on your own gains.

8. Setting unattainable goals

Setting goals for oneself is a powerful and productive action that empowers us to strive for excellence. It is human nature to desire accomplishment and the rewards, which comes after achieving a goal.

However, setting unrealistic goals is counter-productive; often done out of pride or ego. No matter how unachievable or unrealistic, egotists set these goals to internally demonstrate their superiority.

Takeaway: Goals are great but be realistic when constructing them. Further, set mini goals that will provide immediate, actionable things that you can do to achieve the desired outcome.

9. Manipulating others

Egomaniacs not only have high expectations from themselves but they have high expectations from everyone else. They believe they're more intelligent than everyone else, so it could be easy to control them.

When it comes to manipulation and control, egomaniacs are not afraid to throw a compliment or two someone's way to get what they want. They think of it like throwing a bone or an eager dog; the person on the receiving end should be extremely grateful. Mind you, this is all in their head.

Takeaway: Regardless of the situation, don't use manipulation to get what you want. Not only will you likely be unsuccessful, but people will quickly lose trust and respect for you.

Don't try to control your ego, just keep it in pocket and be aware and alert about your behavior in different situations, it will automatically give an idea how to correct yourself on ego level.

ALCOHOL ABUSE

Do you or someone you know have a drinking or drug problem? Learn how to recognize the warning signs and symptoms.

> **"Anyone can give up; it is the easiest thing in the world to do. But to hold it together when everyone would expect you to fall apart, now that is true strength."**
>
> **– Chris Bradford**

Do you have a drinking problem?

It's not always easy to tell when your alcohol intake has crossed the line from moderate or social drinking to problematic drinking. Drinking is so common in many cultures and the effects vary so widely from person to person, it's not always easy to figure out if you have a drinking problem. But if you consume alcohol to cope with difficulties or to avoid feeling bad, you're potentially in dangerous terrain.

You may have a drinking problem if you:

- Feel guilty or ashamed about your drinking.
- Lie to others or hide your drinking habits.
- Need to drink in order to relax or feel better.
- "Black out" or forget what you did while you were drinking.
- Regularly drink more than you intended to.

The bottom line is how alcohol affects you. If your drinking is causing problems in your life, then you have a drinking problem.

Drinking problems can sneak up on you, so it's important to be aware of the warning signs of alcohol abuse and alcoholism and take steps to cut back if you recognize them. Understanding the problem is the first step to overcoming it and either cutting back to healthy levels or quitting altogether.

1. Risk factors for drinking problems and alcoholism

Risk factors for developing problems with alcohol arise from many interconnected factors, including your genetics, how you were raised, your social environment, and your emotional health. People who have a family history of alcoholism or who associate closely with heavy drinkers are more likely to develop drinking problems. Finally, those who suffer from a mental health problem such as anxiety, depression, or bipolar disorder are also particularly at risk, because alcohol is often used to self-medicate.

2. The path from alcohol abuse to alcoholism

Not all alcohol abusers become full-blown alcoholics, but it is a big risk factor. Sometimes alcoholism develops suddenly in response to a stressful change, such as a breakup, retirement, or another loss. Other times, it gradually creeps up on you as your tolerance to alcohol increases. If you're a binge drinker or you drink every day, the risks of developing alcoholism are greater.

Signs And Symptoms Of Alcohol Abuse Or Problem Drinking

Substance abuse experts make a distinction between alcohol abuse and alcoholism (also called alcohol dependence). Unlike alcoholics, alcohol abusers have some ability to set limits on their drinking. However, their alcohol use is still self-destructive and dangerous to themselves or others.

Common signs and symptoms include:

I.   Repeatedly neglecting your responsibilities at home, work, or school because of your drinking. For example, performing poorly at work, flunking classes, neglecting your kids, or skipping out on commitments because you're hung over.

II.   Using alcohol in situations where it's physically dangerous, such as drinking and driving, operating machinery while intoxicated, or mixing alcohol with prescription medication against doctor's orders.

III.   Experiencing repeated legal problems on account of your drinking. For example, getting arrested/penalized for driving under the influence or for drunk and disorderly conduct.

IV.   Continuing to drink even though your alcohol use is causing problems in your relationships. Getting drunk with your buddies, for example, even though you know your wife will be very upset or fighting with your family because they dislike how you act when you drink.

V. Drinking to relax or de-stress. Many drinking problems start when people use alcohol to self-soothe and relieve stress. Getting drunk after every stressful day, for example, or reaching for a bottle every time you have an argument with your spouse or boss.

Signs And Symptoms Of Alcoholism (Alcohol Dependence)

Alcoholism is the most severe form of problem drinking. Alcoholism involves all the symptoms of alcohol abuse, but it also involves another element: physical dependence on alcohol. If you rely on alcohol to function or feel physically compelled to drink, you're an alcoholic.

Tolerance: The 1st major warning sign of alcoholism

Do you have to drink a lot more than you used to in order to get buzzed or to feel relaxed? Can you drink more than other people without getting drunk? These are signs of tolerance, which can be an early warning sign of alcoholism. Tolerance means that, over time, you need more and more alcohol to feel the same effects.

Withdrawal: The 2nd major warning sign

Do you need a drink to steady the shakes in the morning? Drinking to relieve or avoid withdrawal symptoms is a sign of alcoholism and a huge red flag. When you drink heavily, your body gets used to the alcohol and experiences withdrawal symptoms if it's taken away.

Withdrawal symptoms include:

a. Anxiety or jumpiness

b. Shakiness or trembling
c. Sweating
d. Nausea and vomiting
e. Insomnia
f. Depression
g. Irritability
h. Fatigue
i. Loss of appetite
j. Headache

In severe cases, withdrawal from alcohol can also involve hallucinations, confusion, seizures, fever, and agitation. These symptoms can be dangerous, so talk to your doctor if you are a heavy drinker and want to quit.

Other signs and symptoms of alcoholism

- You've lost control over your drinking - You often drink more alcohol than you wanted to, for longer than you intended, or despite telling yourself you wouldn't.
- You want to quit drinking, but you can't - You have a persistent desire to cut down or stop your alcohol use, but your efforts to quit have been unsuccessful.
- You have given up other activities because of alcohol - You're spending less time on activities that used to be important to you (hanging out with family and friends, going to the gym, pursuing your hobbies) because of your alcohol use.
- Alcohol takes up a great deal of your energy and focus - You spend a lot of time drinking, thinking about it, or recovering from its effects. You have few if any interests or social involvements that don't revolve around drinking.
- You drink even though you know it's causing problems - For example, you recognize that your alcohol use is damaging your marriage, making your

depression worse, or causing health problems, but you continue to drink anyway.

Drinking problems and denial

Denial is one of the biggest obstacles to getting help for alcohol abuse and alcoholism. The desire to drink is so strong that the mind finds many ways to rationalize drinking, even when the consequences are obvious. By keeping you from looking honestly at your behavior and its negative effects, denial also exacerbates alcohol-related problems with work, finances, and relationships.

If you have a drinking problem, you may deny it by:

1. Drastically underestimating how much you drink
2. Downplaying the negative consequences of your drinking
3. Complaining that family and friends are exaggerating the problem
4. Blaming your drinking or drinking-related problems on others

For example, you may blame your parents, teachers, an 'unfair boss' for your trouble in studies, grades, at work or a 'nagging wife' for your worrisome marital issues, rather than think about how your drinking is contributing to the problem. While work, relationship, and financial stresses happen to everyone, an overall pattern of deterioration and blaming others may be a sign of trouble.

If you find yourself rationalizing your drinking habits, lying about them, or refusing to discuss the issue, take a moment to consider why you're so defensive. If you truly believe that you don't have a problem, you shouldn't have a reason to cover up your drinking or make excuses.

Five myths about alcoholism and alcohol abuse

Myth: **I can stop drinking anytime I want to.**

Fact: Maybe you can; more likely, you can't. Either way, it's just an excuse to keep drinking. The truth is you don't want to stop. Telling yourself you can quit makes you feel in control, despite all evidence to the contrary and no matter the damage it's causing.

Myth: **My drinking is my problem. I'm the one it hurts, so no one has the right to tell me to stop.**

Fact: It's true that the decision to quit drinking is up to you. But you are deceiving yourself if you think that your drinking hurts no one else but you. Alcoholism affects everyone around you—especially the people closest to you. Your problem is also their problem.

Myth: **I don't drink every day OR I only drink wine or beer, so I can't be an alcoholic.**

Fact: Alcoholism is NOT defined by what you drink, when you drink it, or even how much you drink. It's the EFFECTS of your drinking that define a problem. If your drinking is causing problems in your home or work life, you have a drinking problem—whether you drink daily or only on the weekends, down shots of tequila or stick to wine, drink three bottles of beers a day or three bottles of whiskey.

Myth: **I'm not an alcoholic because I have a job and I'm doing okay.**

Fact: You don't have to be homeless and drinking out of a brown paper bag to be an alcoholic. Many alcoholics can hold down jobs, get through school, and provide for their families. Some are even able to excel. But just because you're a high-functioning alcoholic doesn't mean you're not putting yourself or others in danger. Over time, the effects will catch up with you.

Myth: **Drinking is not a "real" addiction like drug abuse.**

Fact: Alcohol is a drug, and alcoholism is every bit as damaging as drug addiction. Alcohol addiction causes changes in the body and brain, and long-term alcohol abuse can have devastating effects on your health, your career, and your relationships. Alcoholics go through physical withdrawal when they stop drinking, just like drug users experience when they quit.

> *"Courage isn't having the strength to go on – it is going on when you don't have strength."*
>
> *– Napoléon Bonaparte*

Effects Of Alcoholism And Alcohol Abuse

Alcoholism and alcohol abuse can affect all aspects of your life. Long-term alcohol use can cause serious health complications, affecting every organ in your body, including your brain. Problem drinking can also affects your emotional stability, success in academics, finances, career, and your ability to build and sustain satisfying relationships. Alcoholism and alcohol abuse can also have an impact on your family, friends and the people you work with.

The effects of alcohol abuse on the people you love

Despite the potentially lethal damage that heavy drinking inflicts on the body—including cancer, heart problems, and liver disease—the social consequences can be just as devastating than diseases. Alcoholics and alcohol abusers are much more likely to have bad effect on academics, end up with divorce, having problems like domestic violence, struggle for employment, and live in dearth.

But even if you're able to succeed at work or keep your marriage intact, you can't escape from the effects that alcoholism and alcohol abuse have on your personal relationships. Drinking problems put an enormous strain on the people closest to you especially on children.

Often, family members and close friends feel obligated to cover for the person with the drinking problem. So, they take on the burden of cleaning up your messes, lying for you, or working more to make ends meet. Pretending that nothing is wrong and hiding away all their fears and resentments can take an enormous toll. Children are especially sensitive and can suffer long-lasting emotional trauma when a parent or caretaker is an alcoholic or heavy drinker.

> **"Your best days are ahead of you. The movie starts when the guy gets sober and puts his life back together; it doesn't end there."**
>
> **– Bucky Sinister**

Getting help

If you're ready to admit you have a drinking problem, you've already taken the first step. It takes tremendous strength and courage to face alcohol abuse and alcoholism head on. Reaching out for support is the second step.

Whether you choose to go to rehab, rely on self-help programs, get therapy, or take a self-directed treatment approach, support is essential. Recovering from alcohol addiction is much easier when you have people you can lean on for encouragement, comfort, and guidance. Without support, it's easy to fall back into old patterns when the road gets tough.

Your ongoing recovery depends on continuing mental health treatment, learning healthier coping strategies, and making better decisions when dealing with life's challenges. In order to stay alcohol-free for the long term, you'll also have to face the underlying problems that led to your alcoholism or alcohol abuse in the first place.

Those problems could include depression, an inability to manage stress, an unresolved trauma from your childhood, or any number of mental health issues. Such problems may become more prominent when you're no longer using alcohol to cover them up. But you will be in a healthier position to finally address them and seek the help you need.

Helping a loved one

If someone you love has a drinking problem, you may be struggling with a few painful emotions, including shame, fear, anger, and self-blame. The problem may be so overwhelming that it seems easier to ignore it and pretend that nothing is wrong. But in the long run denying it will bring more harm to you, other family members, and the person with the drinking problem.

Reactions to avoid:

Don't make attempt to threaten, punish, bribe, or preach. Avoid emotional appeals that only add to the problem drinker's feelings of guilt and increase their compulsion to drink or use other drugs.

Don't cover up for them or make excuses or shield your loved one from the consequences of their drinking.

Don't take over the problem drinker's responsibilities, leaving them with no sense of importance or dignity.

Don't hide or dump bottles or try to shelter your loved one from situations where alcohol is present.

Don't argue with the person when they are impaired.

Don't drink along with a problem drinker.

Above all, don't feel guilty or responsible for the problem drinker's behavior.

Dealing with a loved one's alcohol problem can feel like an emotional rollercoaster. It's vital that you take care of yourself and get the support you need. It's also important to have people you can talk honestly and openly with about what you're going through.

A good place to start is by joining a group such as Al-Anon, a free peer support group for families coping with alcoholism. Listening to others with the same challenges can serve as a tremendous source of comfort and support. You can also turn to trusted friends, a therapist, or people in your faith community.

You cannot force someone you love to stop alcohol consumption. As much as you may want to, and as hard as it is to watch, you cannot make someone stop drinking. The choice is up to them.

Don't expect the person to stop drinking and stay sober without help. Your loved one will need treatment, support, and new coping skills to overcome a serious drinking problem.

Recovery is an ongoing process. Recovery is a bumpy road, requiring time and patience. An alcoholic will not magically become a different person once sober. And the problems that led to the alcohol abuse in the first place will have to be faced.

Admitting that there's a serious problem can be painful for the whole family, not just the alcohol abuser. But don't be ashamed. You're not alone. Alcoholism and alcohol abuse affect millions of families, from every social class, race, and culture. But there is help and support available for both you and your loved one.

When your teen has a drinking problem

Finding out that your child is drinking can generate fear, confusion, and anger in parents. It's important to remain calm when confronting your teen, and only do so when everyone is sober. Explain your concerns and make it clear that your concern comes from a place of love. It's important that your teen feels you are supportive.

Steps parents can take:

Encode rules and consequences: Your teen should understand that drinking alcohol comes with specific consequences. But don't make hollow threats or set rules that you cannot enforce. Make sure your spouse agrees with the rules and is prepared to enforce them.

Monitor your teen's activity: Know where your teen goes and who they hang out with. Remove or lock away alcohol from your home and routinely check potential hiding places for alcohol—in backpacks, under the bed, between clothes in a drawer, for example. Explain to your teen that this lack of privacy is a consequence of having been caught using alcohol.

Encourage other interests and social activities. Expose your teen to healthy hobbies and activities, such as team sports, Scouts, and after-school clubs.

Talk to your child about underlying issues. Drinking could be the result of other problems. Is your child having trouble fitting in? Has there been a recent major change, like a move or divorce, which is causing stress?

Get outside help: You don't have to go it alone. Teenagers often rebel against their parents but if they hear the same information from a different authority figure, they may be more inclined to listen. Try seeking help from a sports coach, family doctor, therapist, or counselor.

Next step: Finding the right alcohol addiction treatment

Many effective alcohol treatment options are available, including rehab programs. However, professional help isn't the only way to overcome the problem and recover. There are also plenty of steps you can take to help yourself stop drinking, achieve lasting recovery, and regain control of your life.

DRUG ABUSE AND ADDICTION

Do you or someone you know have a drug problem? Explore the warning signs and symptoms and learn how substance abuse problems develop.

> *"Recovery is hard. Regret is harder."*
>
> *– Brittany Burgunder*

When does drug use become drug abuse or addiction?

People from all walks of life can experience problems with their drug use, regardless of age, race, background, or the reason they started using drugs in the first place. Some people experiment with recreational drugs out of curiosity, to have a good time, because friends are doing it, or to ease problems such as stress, anxiety, or depression. However, it's not just illegal drugs, such as cocaine or heroin, that can lead to abuse and addiction.

Prescription medications such as painkillers, sleeping pills, and tranquilizers can cause similar problems. In fact, next to marijuana, prescription painkillers are the most abused drugs in the U.S. and more people die from overdosing powerful opioid painkillers each day than from traffic accidents and gun deaths combined. And addiction to opioid painkillers can be so powerful it has become the major risk factor for heroin abuse.

Of course, drug use—either illegal or prescription—doesn't automatically lead to abuse. Some people can use recreational or prescription drugs without experiencing negative effects, while others find that substance use takes a serious toll on their health and well-being. Similarly, there is no specific point at which drug use moves from casual to problematic.

Drug abuse and addiction is less about the type or amount of the substance consumed or the frequency of your drug use, and more about the consequences of that drug use. If your drug use is causing problems in your life—at work, school, home, or in your relationships—you likely have a drug abuse or addiction problem.

If you're worried about drug use your own or a loved one, learning how drug abuse and addiction develops—and why it can have such a powerful hold—will give you a better understanding of how to best deal with the problem and regain control of your life. Recognizing that you have a problem is the first step on the road to recovery, one that takes tremendous courage and strength. Facing your problem without minimizing the issue or making excuses can feel frightening and overwhelming, but recovery is within reach. If you're ready to seek help, you can overcome your addiction and build a satisfying, drug-free life for yourself.

How Drug Abuse And Addiction Develop

A thin line lies between regular drug use and drug abuse/addiction. Very few drug abusers or addicts can recognize when they've crossed that line. While frequency or the number of drugs consumed do not necessarily constitute drug abuse or addiction, they can often be indicators of drug-related problems.

If the drug fulfills a valuable need, you may find yourself increasingly relying on it. You may take illegal drugs to calm or energize yourself or make you more confident. You may start abusing prescription drugs to relieve pain, cope with panic attacks, or improve concentration at school or work. If you are using drugs to fill a void in your life, you're more at risk of crossing the line from casual drug use to drug abuse and addiction. To maintain a healthy balance in your life, you need to have positive experiences and feel good about your life without any drug use.

Drug abuse may start due to social connects. People often try drugs for the first time in social situations with friends and acquaintances. A strong desire to fit in to the group, it makes the person using drugs to realize that it could be the only option.

Problems can sometimes sneak on your thinking, as your drug use gradually increases over time. Smoking a joint with friends over the weekend, or taking ecstasy at a rave party, or painkillers when your back aches, are the examples, that can change from using drugs a couple of days a week to using them every day. Gradually, getting and using the drug becomes more and more often will be necessity to you.

As drug abuse takes hold, you may miss or frequently be late for work or school, your job performance may progressively deteriorate, and you may start to neglect social or family responsibilities. Your ability to stop using is eventually compromised.

What began as a voluntary choice has turned into a physical and psychological necessity?

Eventually drug abuse will consume your life, stops social and intellectual development. This only reinforces feelings of isolation.

> **"Success is the sum of small efforts, repeated day in and day out."**
>
> **– Robert Collier**

DEPRESSION, ANXIETY, BIPOLAR DISORDER

> *"Mental pain is less dramatic than physical pain, but it is more common and also harder to bear. The frequent attempt to conceal mental pain increases the burden: it is easier to say "My tooth is aching" than to say "My heart is broken."*
>
> — *C.S. Lewis, The Problem of Pain*

Common signs and symptoms of depression

1. Feelings of helplessness and hopelessness.
2. Loss of interest in daily activities.
3. Inability to experience pleasure.
4. Appetite or weight changes.
5. Sleep changes.
6. Loss of energy.
7. Strong feelings of worthlessness or guilt.
8. Concentration problems.
9. Anger, physical pain, and reckless behavior (especially in men).
10. Common signs and symptoms of anxiety.
11. Excessive tension and worry.
12. Feeling restless or jumpy.
13. Irritability or feeling "on edge".
14. Racing heart or shortness of breath.
15. Nausea, trembling, or dizziness.
16. Muscle tension, headaches.
17. Trouble concentrating.
18. Insomnia.

Common sign and symptoms of mania in bipolar disorder

1. Feelings of euphoria or extreme irritability.
2. Unrealistic, grandiose beliefs.
3. Decreased need for sleep.
4. Increased energy.
5. Rapid speech and racing thoughts.
6. Impaired judgment and impulsivity.
7. Hyperactivity.
8. Anger or rage.

> *"Our greatest glory is not in never failing, but in rising up every time we fail."*
>
> *– Ralph Waldo Emerson*

Keep in mind:

There is always hope. Both mood swings and alcohol/drug abuse problems are treatable conditions. Recovering from co-occurring disorders takes time, commitment, and courage, but people with substance abuse and mental health problems can and do get better.

It's important to get and stay sober during treatment. If your doctor needs to prescribe medication for your mental health problem, mixing it with alcohol or drugs could have serious consequences. Similarly, talk therapy is less effective, if you're under the influence of drugs or alcohol.

Relapses are part of the recovery process. Don't get too discouraged if you relapse. Slips and setbacks happen, but, with hard work, most people can recover from their relapses and move on with recovery.

Peer support could be helpful. You may be benefited from joining a self-help support group. A support group gives you a chance to lean on others who know exactly what you're going through and learn from their experiences.

How To Find The Right Program For Co-Occurring Disorders

Make sure that the program is appropriately licensed and accredited. The treatment methods are backed by research, and there is an aftercare program to prevent relapse. Additionally, you should make sure that the program has designed for issues concerning with mental health issue. Some programs, for example, may have experience treating depression or anxiety, but not schizophrenia or bipolar disorder.

There are a variety of approaches that treatment programs may take, but there are some basics of effective treatment that you should look for:

Treatment addresses both the substance abuse problem and your mental health problem.

You share in the decision-making process and are actively involved in setting goals and developing strategies for change.

Treatment includes basic education about your disorder and related problems.

You are taught healthy coping skills and strategies to minimize substance abuse, strengthen your relationships, and cope with life's stressors, challenges, and upset.

Treatment for dual diagnosis or co-occurring disorders

Can help you to:

Think about the role that alcohol and/or drugs play in your life. This should be done confidentially, without judgement or any negative consequences. People feel free to discuss these issues when the discussion is confidential and not tied to legal consequences.

Learn more about alcohol and drugs, such as how they interact with mental illness and medication.

Become employed and find other services that may help the process of recovery.

Identify and develop your personal recovery goals. If you decide that your use of alcohol or drugs may be a problem, a counselor trained in dual diagnosis treatment can help you work on your specific recovery goals for both illnesses.

Experience counseling specifically designed for people with dual diagnosis. This can be done individually, in a group of peers, with your family, or a combination of all these.

Treatment programs for veterans with co-occurring disorders

Veterans deal with additional challenges when it comes to co-occurring disorders. The pressures of deployment or combat can exacerbate underlying mental disorders, and substance abuse is a common way of coping with unpleasant feelings or memories. Often, these problems take a while to show up after a vet returns home and may be initially mistaken for readjustment. Untreated co-occurring disorders can lead to major problems at home and work and in your daily life, so it's important to seek help.

"Character cannot be developed in ease and quiet. Only through experience of trial and suffering can

> *the soul be strengthened, ambition inspired, and success achieved."*
> *– Helen Keller*

Self-Help For Substance Abuse And Co-Occurring Disorders

In addition to getting professional treatment, there are plenty of self-help steps that you can take to address your substance abuse and mental health issues. Remember, getting sober is only the beginning. As well as continuing mental health treatment, your sustained recovery depends on learning healthier coping strategies and making better decisions when dealing with life's challenges.

Recovery tip 1: Recognize and manage overwhelming stress and emotions

Learn how to manage stress - Drug and alcohol abuse often stem up from misguided attempts to manage stress. Stress is an inevitable part of life, so it's important to have healthy coping skills so you can deal with stress without turning to alcohol or drugs. Stress management skills go a long way towards preventing relapse and keeping your symptoms at bay.

Cope with unpleasant feelings - Many people turn to alcohol or drugs to cover up painful memories and emotions such as loneliness, depression, or anxiety. You may feel like doing drugs is the only way to handle unpleasant feelings but Help Guide's free Emotional Intelligence Toolkit and spiritual practices, regular interaction with counsellor teach you how to cope with difficult emotions without falling back on your addiction.

Know your triggers and have an action plan - When you're coping with a mental disorder as well as a substance abuse problem, it's especially important to know signs that your illness is flaring up. Common causes include stressful events, big life changes, or unhealthy sleeping or eating patterns. At these times, having a plan in place is essential to preventing a drink or drug relapse. Who will you talk to? What do you need to do to avoid slipping?

Recovery tip 2: Stay connected to others

Make face-to-face connection with friends and family a priority - Positive emotional connection to those around you is the quickest way to calm your nervous system. Try to meet up regularly with people who care about you. If you don't have anyone you feel close to, it's never too late to meet new people and develop meaningful friendships.

Follow doctor's orders - Once you are sober and you feel better, you might think you no longer need medication or treatment. But arbitrarily stopping medication or treatment is a common reason for relapse in people with co-occurring disorders. Always talk with your doctor before making any changes to your medication or treatment routine.

Get therapy or stay involved in a support group - Your chances of staying sober improve if you are participating in a social support group or if you are getting therapy.

Recovery tip 3: Make healthy lifestyle changes

Exercise regularly - Exercise is a natural way to bust stress, relieve anxiety, and improve your mood and outlook. To achieve the maximum benefit, aim for at least 30 minutes of aerobic exercise on most days.

Practice relaxation techniques - When practiced regularly, relaxation techniques such as mindfulness meditation, progressive muscle relaxation, and deep breathing can reduce symptoms of stress, anxiety, and depression, and increase feelings of relaxation and emotional well-being.

Adopt healthy eating habits - Start the day right with breakfast and continue with frequent small meals throughout the day. Going too long without eating leads to low blood sugar, which can make you feel more stressed or anxious. Getting enough healthy fats in your diet can help to boost your mood.

Get enough sleep - A lack of sleep can exacerbate stress, anxiety, and depression, so try to get 7 to 9 hours of quality sleep a night.

Recovery tip 4: Make healthy lifestyle changes

To stay from alcohol or drug for the long term, you need to build a new, meaningful life where substance abuse no longer has a place.

Develop new activities and interests - Find new hobbies, volunteer activities, or work that gives you a sense of meaning and purpose. When you're doing things you find fulfilling, you'll feel better about yourself and substance use will hold less appeal.

Avoid the things that trigger your urge to consume alcohol/drugs - If certain people, places, or activities trigger a craving for drugs or alcohol, try to avoid them. This may mean making major changes to your social life, such as finding new things to do with your old buddies—or even giving up those friends and making new connections.

Group Support For Substance Abuse And Co-Occurring Disorders

As like other addictions, groups are very helpful, not only in maintaining sobriety, but also as a safe place to get support and discuss challenges. Sometimes treatment programs for co-occurring disorders provide groups that continue to meet on an aftercare basis. Your doctor or treatment provider may also be able to refer you to a group for people with co-occurring disorders.

While it's often best to join a group that addresses both substance abuse and your mental health disorder, twelve-step groups for substance abuse can also be helpful—plus they're more common, so you're likely to find one in your area. These free programs, facilitated by peers, use group support and a set of guided principles—the twelve steps—to obtain and maintain sobriety.

Just make sure your group is accepting of the idea of co-occurring disorders and psychiatric medication. Some people in these groups, although well meaning, may mistake taking psychiatric medication as another form of addiction. You want a place to feel safe, not pressured.

Helping a loved one with a substance abuse and mental health problem

Helping a loved one from both a substance abuse and a mental health problem could be a roller coaster. Resistance to treatment is common and the road to recovery can be long.

The best way to help someone is to accept what you can and cannot do. You cannot force someone to remain sober, nor can you make someone take their medication or keep appointments. What you can do is make positive choices for yourself, encourage your loved one to get help, and offer your support while making sure you don't lose yourself in the process.

Seek support - Dealing with a loved one's mental illness and substance abuse can be painful and isolating. Make sure you're getting the emotional support you need to cope. Talk to someone you trust about what you're going through. It can also help to get your own therapy or join a support group.

Set boundaries - Be realistic about the amount of care you're able to provide without feeling overwhelmed and resentful. Set limits on disruptive behaviors and stick to them. Letting the co-occurring disorders take over your life isn't healthy for you or your loved one.

Educate yourself - Learn all you can do for your loved one's mental health problem and substance abuse treatment or recovery. The more you understand what your loved one is going through, the better able you'll be to support recovery.

Be patient - Recovering from co-occurring disorders doesn't happen overnight. Recovery is an ongoing process and relapse is common. Ongoing support for both you and your loved one is crucial as you work toward recovery, but you can get through this difficult time together and regain control of your lives.

GRATITUDE IN ATTITUDE

Gratitude and its associate appreciation are the mental tool we use to remind ourselves of the good stuff. It's a lens that helps us to see the things that don't make it onto our lists of problems to be solved. It's a spotlight that we shine on the people who give us the good things in life. It's a bright red paintbrush we apply to otherwise-invisible blessings, like clean streets or health or enough food to eat.

Gratitude doesn't make problems and threats disappear. We can fail in exam, lose chance to get admission to college of reputation and liking, lose job, we can get sick. The threats are indeed real, but at that moment, they exist only in memory or imagination. I am the threat; it is me who is wearing myself out with worry.

That's when I need to turn on the gratitude. If I do that enough, suggests the psychological research, gratitude might just become a habit. What will that mean for me? It means, says the research, that I increase my chances of psychologically surviving hard times, that I stand a chance to be happier in the good times. I'm not ignoring the threats; I'm appreciating the resources and people that might help me face those threats.

Steps To Develop Gratitude

- Occasionally, think about death and loss

Realize that death is going to come sooner or later, you will immediately start feeling gratuitous about life and whatever you have, you will be thankful to god. See what's happening due to corona virus, lot of people have gone down big financially in share market no one could have imagined, at least you are not facing such financial crisis or even if you are facing, you are losing your life like many have lost due to corona virus.

•   Remind yourself of absence of things which you take for granted: it is natural that we lose importance of things which become part of our life regularly. Well, we humans are astoundingly adaptive creatures, and we will adapt even to the good things. When we do, their subjective value starts to drop; we start to take them for granted. That's the point at which we might give them up for a while—be it chocolate, sex, or even something like sunlight—and then take the time to really savor them when we allow them back into our lives.

That goes for people, too, and that goes back to the first habit: If you're taking someone for granted, take a step back—and imagine your life without them. Then try savoring their presence, just like you would a rose. Or a new car. Whatever! The point is absence may just make the heart grow grateful.

You might also consider adding some little ritual to how you experience the pleasures of the body: A study published this year in Psychological Science finds that rituals like prayer or even just shaking a sugar packet "make people pay more attention to food, and paying attention makes food taste better," as Emily Nauman reports in her Greater Good article about the research.

1.   They take the good things as gifts, not birthrights

What's the opposite of gratitude? Entitlement—the attitude that people owe you something just because you're so very special.

"In all its manifestations, a preoccupation with the self can cause us to forget our benefits and our benefactors or to feel that we are owed things from others and therefore have no reason to feel thankful, "Counting blessings will be ineffective because grievances will always outnumber gifts.""

The antidote to entitlement, argues Emmons, is to see that we did not create ourselves—we were created, if not by evolution, then by God, or if not by God, then by our parents. Likewise, we are never truly self-sufficient. Humans need other people to grow our food and heal our injuries; we need love, and for that we need family, partners, friends, and pets.

"Seeing with grateful eyes requires that we see the web of interconnection in which we alternate between being givers and receivers, "The humble person says that life is a gift to be grateful for, not a right to be claimed.""

2.   They're grateful to people, not just things:

Experiences that heighten meaningful connections with others—like noticing how another person has helped you, acknowledging the effort it took, and savoring how you benefitted from it—engage biological systems for trust and affection, alongside circuits for pleasure and reward. This provides a synergistic and enduring boost to the positive experience. Saying 'thank you' to a person, your brain registers that something good has happened and that you are more richly enmeshed in a meaningful social community.

3.   Show gratitude with love and care, it should not be just superficial.

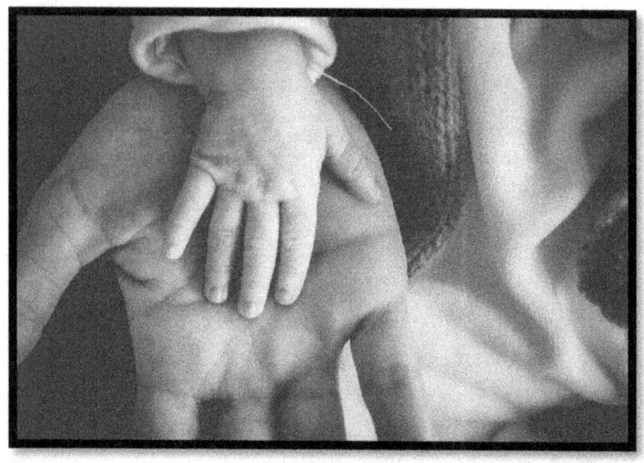

4. They thank outside the box

"Life is suffering. No amount of positive thinking exercises will change this truth."

So, telling people simply to buck up, count their blessings, and remember how much they still must be grateful for can certainly do much harm. Processing a life experience through a grateful lens does not mean denying negativity. It is not a form of superficial happiology. Instead, it means realizing the power you must transform an obstacle into an opportunity. It means reframing a loss into a potential gain, recasting negativity into positive channels for gratitude.

How Gratitude Changes You and Your Brain

"New research is starting to explore how gratitude works to improve our mental health."

-Joel Wong, Joshua Brown

With the rise of managed health care, which emphasizes cost-efficiency and brevity, mental health professionals have had to confront this burning question: How can they help clients derive the greatest possible benefit from treatment in the shortest amount of time?

Recent evidence suggests that a promising approach is to complement psychological counseling with additional activities that are not too taxing for clients but yield high results. In our own research, we have zeroed in on one such activity: the practice of gratitude. Indeed, many studies over the past decade have found that people who consciously count their blessings tend to be happier and less depressed.

The problem is that most research studies on gratitude have been conducted with well-functioning people. Is gratitude beneficial for people who struggle with mental health concerns? And, if so, how?

We set out to address these questions in a recent research study involving nearly 300 adults, mostly college students who were seeking mental health counseling at a university. We recruited these participants just before they began their first session of counseling, and, on average, they reported clinically low levels of mental health at the time. Many people seeking counseling services at this university in general struggled with issues related to depression and anxiety.

What did we find? Compared with the participants who wrote about negative experiences or only received counseling, those who wrote gratitude letters reported significantly better mental health four weeks and 12 weeks after their writing exercise ended. This suggests that gratitude writing can be beneficial not just for healthy, well-adjusted individuals, but also for those who struggle with mental health concerns. In fact, it seems, practicing gratitude on top of receiving psychological counseling carries greater benefits than counseling alone, even when that gratitude practice is brief.

HOW TO OVERCOME SUICIDAL TENDENCIES

> **"Suicide doesn't end the pain; it passes to the ones you love and remains."**

Every person has different definition of success and happiness, but if you ask me, I would always say, it is the time when you take out someone from their suicidal tendencies, depression, anxiety, that is the most satisfying point in life. I did this with many youngsters and will continue to do it. My experience tells me that if you have belongingness, love, conviction, spiritual base, it's not a difficult task to bring them out from trouble they are encountering. Whatever we discussed till now and going to discuss further, will surely help to come out of these issues a person is facing.

Let's understand sequence in life and suicidal tendencies:

We're going to use the analogy of a play, as in a theatre production. When you incarnate you pick your parents and life circumstances? You are, in effect, accepting a role in a play. A lot of behind the scenes work goes into creating your role in this play. Other people may have wanted the role, but you got it. Now you're responsible for what you do with it.

So, you incarnate and you're doing your part just fine. Then one day you find that the play is getting harder and harder to perform. Maybe you're late for a performance. Maybe you don't like the lines you're getting. Maybe the audience is heckling you. Maybe your role is just tough; you're in every scene, and you don't feel like you have a chance to catch your breath. Maybe you're in no scenes and you're starting to feel ignored or like nobody cares. Maybe you don't like your fellow actors. Maybe someone else in the play is hurting you. For whatever reason, the role you've got just doesn't make you happy any longer and you want to quit.

Let's understand this way, if someone insults you badly when you are with your close friends or loved ones. What happens for rest of the day, it goes on in mind again and again, causing stress and feel depressed. Before sleep, same thoughts are running through your mind, then you sleep, wake up the in the morning. Which thoughts come first immediately after waking up?? The same thoughts which were going through your mind before sleep, will again resurface in your mind. It means our memory stores strong impressions mostly disturbances in our mind. So, when someone is in state of suicidal tendency, their mind is full of disturbances, stress, pressure, negativity, distrust, low on confidence and positive vibration. suicide at this state, soul carries the same negative impressions in next life, what does it say, next life would be more stressful, difficult than the current one. It's like taking out your clothes when you are in -60 degrees Celsius environment. Why to put our life in more dangerous situation than in the present situation.

I know life can seem tough sometimes. Most of the people have contemplated suicide at some point in their lives. Sometimes life seems overwhelmingly hard. But you can change your life any time you want. Whatever you've gotten yourself into, there's a way out that doesn't involve quitting. You may get to the end of your life completely worn out, broken, and even devastated, but from a spiritual perspective that's better than quitting. When you quit you still must learn all the lessons you came here to learn, so the next time you incarnate it isn't going to get easier, it will probably be harder.

Don't quit the play. Ask for help. Maybe you can be sent them on vacation and your colleague can perform your role for a while. Maybe you can get the writers to give you fewer lines, or more support in your scenes. But don't quit. People are counting on you, including your higher self. God only gives you as much as you can handle, but sometimes it's hard to remember how strong you really are. You're allowed to ask for help. God gives you that too … when you ask for it. Accept the help when it comes.

Some people think that near and dear ones will have sympathy for them after their suicide, what's the use of such sympathy when you are not going to feel it? So, this emotional thinking is meaningless after your suicide.

Who suffers most? It is your parents or near and dear ones, I want to ask youngsters, you want to lose your life for any boy or girl to whom you know for few months or years, have you ever thought of your parents, struggling just to see best version of yourself and want to see you always happy and most important , they are doing it out of love, without any expectation or selfish motive. Can you imagine, what will happen to them if you go out suddenly from their life?? It would be the most difficult phase of their life, no one could ever imagine. Do you want your parents to suffer?? Think, think, Think…

There are millions of people on earth, if someone reject you, does it mean you don't have other options available, it's better to move on in life than taking extreme steps. Same thing about grades in exam.

So, what if you scoreless in an exam or failed, there will be many more exams in future, work for it.

So, what you are not physically smart enough or have some deficiency, if you see many big successful personalities, they are not good looking, success doesn't depend how good looking you are but depends on inner virtues.

DON'T QUIT

When things go wrong, as they sometimes will,

When the road you're trudging seems all uphill,

When the funds are low, and debts are high,

And you want to smile, but you have to sigh.

When all is pressing you down a bit-

Rest if you must, but don't you quit.

Success is failure turned inside out,

The silver tint in the clouds of doubt,

And you never can tell how close you are,

It might be near when it seems far.

So, stick to the fight when your hardest hit-

It's when things seem worst that you must not Quit.

-    John G. Whittier

Suicide, is an act of taking your own life, is a tragic reaction to stressful life situations — and even more tragic because suicide can be prevented. Whether you're considering to commit suicide or know someone who have suicidal tendencies, learn signs of suicidal tendencies and how to reach out for immediate help and professional treatment. You may save a life — your own or someone else's.

It may seem like there's no way to solve your problems and that suicide is the only way to end the pain. But you can take steps to stay safe — and start enjoying your life again

Symptoms

Suicide warning signs or suicidal thoughts include:

❖ Talking about committing suicide — for example, making statements such as "I'm going to kill myself," "I wish I were dead," or "I wish I hadn't been born".

❖ Procuring the means to take your own life, such as buying a gun or stockpiling pills.

❖ Withdrawing from social contacts and wanting to be left alone.

❖ Having mood swings, such as being emotionally high one day and deeply discouraged the next.

❖ Being preoccupied with death, dying or violence.

❖ Feeling trapped or hopeless about a situation.

❖ Increasing use of alcohol or drugs.

❖ Changing normal routine, including eating or sleeping patterns.

❖ Doing risky or self-destructive things, such as using drugs or driving recklessly.

❖ Giving away belongings or getting affairs in order when there's no other logical explanation for doing this.

❖ Saying goodbye to people as if they won't be seen again.

❖ Developing personality changes or being severely anxious or agitated, particularly when experiencing some of the warning signs listed above.

Warning signs aren't always obvious, and they may vary from person to person. Some people make their intentions clear, while others keep suicidal thoughts and feelings secret.

When to see a doctor

If you're feeling suicidal, but you aren't immediately thinking of hurting yourself:

Reach out to a close friend or loved one — even though it may be hard to talk about your feelings

Contact an authority, spiritual leader or someone in your faith community

Call a suicide hotline

Make an appointment with your doctor, other health care provider or a mental health professional

> *"Suicidal thinking doesn't get better on its own — so get help."*

Risk Factors

Although suicide attempts are more frequent and common in women. Men are more likely to be successful in their act of committing suicide rather than women because men typically use more-lethal methods, such as a firearm.

You may be at risk of suicide if you:

Attempted suicide before,

Feel hopeless, worthless, agitated, socially isolated or lonely,

Experience a stressful life event, such as the loss of a loved one, military service, a breakup, or financial or legal problems,

Have a substance abuse problem — alcohol and drug abuse can worsen thoughts of suicide and make you feel reckless or impulsive enough to act on your thoughts,

Have suicidal thoughts and have access to firearms in your home,

Have an underlying psychiatric disorder, such as major depression, post-traumatic stress disorder or bipolar disorder,

Have a family history of mental disorders, substance abuse, suicide, or violence, including physical or sexual abuse,

Have a medical condition that can be linked to depression and suicidal thinking, such as chronic disease, chronic pain or terminal illness,

Are lesbian, gay, bisexual or transgender with an unsupportive family or in a hostile environment,

❚ *"Where there is life there is hope."*

Children and teenagers

Suicide in children and teenagers can followed by stressful life events. What a young person sees as serious and insurmountable may seem minor to an adult — such as problems in school or the loss of a friendship. In some cases, a child or teen may feel suicidal due to certain life circumstances that he or she may not want to talk about, such as:

Having a psychiatric disorder, including depression

Loss or conflict with close friends or family members

History of physical or sexual abuse

Problems with alcohol or drugs

Physical or medical issues, for example, becoming pregnant or having a sexually transmitted infection

Being the victim of bullying

Being uncertain of sexual orientation

Reading or hearing an account of suicide or knowing a peer who died by suicide

If you have concerns about a friend or family member, asking about suicidal thoughts and intentions is the best way to identify risk.

Prevention

To help keep yourself from feeling suicidal:

Get the treatment you need. If you don't treat the underlying cause, your suicidal thoughts are likely to return. You may feel embarrassed to seek treatment for mental health problems, but getting the right treatment for depression, substance misuse or another underlying problem will make you feel better about life — and help keep you safe.

Establish your support network. It may be hard to talk about suicidal feelings, and your friends and family may not fully understand why you feel the way you do. Reach out anyway, and make sure the people who care about you know what's going on and are there when you need them. You may also want to get help from your place of worship, support groups or other community resources. Feeling connected and supported can help reduce suicide risk.

Remember, suicidal feelings are temporary. If you feel hopeless or that life's not worth living anymore, remember that treatment can help you regain your perspective — and life will get better. Take one step at a time and don't act impulsively.

> *"Life is like a game of chess.*
>
> *To win you have to make a move.*
>
> *Knowing which move to make comes with IN-SIGHT*
>
> *and knowledge, and by learning the lessons that are*
>
> *acculated along the way.*
>
> *We become each and every piece within the game called life!"*
>
> *"Life is like a sandwich!*
>
> *Birth as one slice,*
>
> *and death as the other.*
>
> *What you put in-between*
>
> *the slices is up to you.*
>
> *Is your sandwich tasty or sour?*
>
> *— Allan Rufus, The Master's Sacred Knowledge*

SEVA
(SELFLESS SERVICE)

Many problems in our society is linked with our thinking and attitude. Greed, only me attitude, results in depression, life seems to be burden, boring and so on…

Nature loves to give out whatever it has selflessly to all the living beings. Only human being works opposite to the nature, it always thinks of himself and that greed destroys environment and other living beings on the planet earth, brings out misery to self and disturbed life.

Have you ever experienced happiness when you help someone selflessly? Our consciousness expands and we feel joyous, that's the beauty of our consciousness and nature. Sharing and caring attitude developed at the growing age will surely bring good fortunes and stability in bad times. When you work in synchronism with nature, nature takes care of you in a best possible way. I am not saying you give out everything you earned but little part of it for under privileged.

It is not only about money but motivating someone when they are not in a good mood, planting trees, stopping wastage of natural resources, giving shoulder to someone who is emotionally broken down. If you are depressed someday, just go out and help someone, Selfless service will automatically lift your mood. Whatever you give to society, it will come back to you in same fashion immediately or some other time in different way. Karma never misses any opportunity to give back in same fashion.

Research indicates numerous benefits to those who engage in selfless service, including reduction of emotional disturbance, greater longevity, stress reduction, improved morale, increased self-confidence and self-esteem, better health and pain reduction, and greater overall happiness. According to Spiritual Guru Sri Sri Ravi Shankar ji, the joy of giving is far more exhilarating than the joy of getting and can be likened to a thrill or high.

> *"The strongest people make time to help others, even when they are struggling themselves."*
>
> *"A selfless service to humanity is also a selfless service to God."*
>
> *"The best way to find yourself is to lose yourself in the service of others."*

Cycle of Karma (SEVA)

Once a highly successful businessman, running a health insurance company was getting ready to go to his office. When he reached into his car and opened a door, a stray dog sleeping under his car suddenly came out and bit on his leg! The businessman got very angry and quickly picked up a few rocks and threw at the dog, but none hit the dog. The dog ran away.

Upon reaching his office, the businessman calls a meeting of his managers and during the meeting he puts the anger of dog on them. The managers also get upset by the anger of their boss and they put their anger to the employees working under them. The chain of this reaction keeps going till the lower level of employees and finally, the anger reaches to the office peon.

Now, there was no one working under the peon! So, after the office time is over, he reaches his home, and wife opens the door. She asked him, "Why are you so late today?" The peon upset due to anger threw at him by the staff, gives one slap to his wife! And says, "I didn't go to the office to play football, I went to work so don't irritate me with your stupid questions!"

So, now the wife got upset that she got a scolding plus a slap for no reason. She puts her anger on his son who was watching tv and give him a slap, "This is all you do, you have no interest in studying! Turn off the TV now!"

The son gets upset now! He walks out of his house and sees a dog passing by looking at him. He picks up a rock and hits the dog in his anger and frustration. The dog, getting hit by a rock, runs away barking in pain.

This was the same dog that bit the businessman early morning.

Moral of the story:

No one can run away from cycle of Karma. Harvest as one has sown. This is how the life works. While we all worry about hell and heaven based on our deeds, we should focus more on how we are living and behaving. Do good, Good will come, do bad, bad will come.

❚ *"Purify the mind through selfless service."*

FOOD – THE MEDICINE

L ot of people on planet earth have misconception that whatever food we eat is just to gain energy. Energy (Positive) is one of the aspects, but food also has strong impact on the functioning of our mind and intellect, metabolic reactions and overall digestion system, many diseases are result of our bad food habits. Even whatever diseases has come out till today, like corona virus, a deadly one, reason for huge number of deaths, millions are suffering in the whole world, damaged world economy, creating havoc everywhere, is basically due to bad habit of food. Our careless and selfish attitude is destroying the nature badly and the reverse effect is everyone is suffering.

> **"Killing animals to satisfy a tongue is the worst think mankind has chosen."**

- Animals require huge amount of food grains to develop the flesh required for the human being to eat, the same food grain can help in alleviating poverty and even the inflation can be brought down.

- It also badly impacts total environment, soil, water, air is polluted to large extend resulting in global warming. What type of environment we want to leave for our future generations?? Methane gas produced during burping and chirping by animals is almost 20% harmful than carbon dioxide. Huge amount of water is wasted daily to convert animal into meat. Soil pollution is another factor.

- Non-vegetarian food comes under the category of "Tamsik food", which badly affects mind and intellect in long run. Aggression, violence like traits can develop in such persons.

- Many Researchers are saying that it is carcinogenic. Many cancers especially related to digestive system are linked to non-vegetarian food. Diabetes blood pressure and heart diseases are linked in many cases.

The food we eat gives our bodies the "information" and materials they need to function properly. If we don't get the right information, our metabolic processes suffer and our health declines.

If we get too much food, or food that gives our bodies the wrong instructions, we can become overweight, undernourished, and at risk for the development of diseases and conditions, such as arthritis, diabetes, and heart disease.

In short, what we eat is central to our health. Considering Webster's definition of medicine: "The science and art dealing with the maintenance of health and the prevention, alleviation, or cure of disease."

Food acts as medicine--to maintain, prevent, and treat disease.

What does food do in our bodies?

"Nutrients are the nourishing substances in food that are essential for the growth, development and maintenance of body functions. Essential meaning that if a nutrient is not present, aspects of function and therefore human health decline. When nutrient intake does not regularly meet the nutrient needs dictated by the cell activity, the metabolic processes slow down or even stop."

In other words, nutrients give our bodies instructions about how to function. In this sense, food be a source of "information" for the body.

Thinking about food in this way gives us a view of nutrition that goes beyond calories or grams, good foods or bad foods. This view leads us to focus on foods we should include rather than foods to exclude.

Instead of viewing food as the enemy, we look to food to create health and reduce disease by helping the body maintain function.

The food you eat can affect your health and your protect against risk from certain diseases. To eat healthier food, you may need to change some of your daily habits. You also may need to change some things in your environment. Your environment includes everything around you, like your home or the place you work.

You don't need to make huge changes to eat healthier. And you don't have to change your habits all at the same time. It's best to set small goals and change your habits a little bit at a time. Over time, small changes can make a big difference in your health.

This information will help you make useful changes for healthy eating.

Changing your eating habits and your environment can help you eat healthier foods.

A healthy diet is good for your overall health. It also can help you reach a healthy weight and stay there.

To improve your eating habits, it's best to make small lifestyle changes that you can keep doing over time.

How can you change your eating habits?

To eat a healthy diet, you may need to make some changes. Remember that you can change your eating habits a little bit at a time. Small changes are easier to make and can lead to better health.

Here are some ways to make healthy changes in your eating habits:

Keep more fruits, low-fat dairy products (low-fat milk and low-fat yogurt), vegetables, and whole-grain foods at home and at work. Focus on adding healthy food to your diet, rather than just taking unhealthy foods away.

Try to eat a family meal every day at the kitchen or dining table. This will help you focus on eating healthy meals.

Pack a healthy lunch and snacks for work. This lets you have more control over what you eat.

Put your snacks on a plate instead of eating from the package. This helps you control how much you eat.

Don't skip or delay meals and be sure to schedule your snacks. If you ignore your feelings of hunger, you may end up eating too much or choosing an unhealthy snack. If you often feel too hungry, it can cause you to focus a lot on food.

Eat your meals with others whenever you could. Relax and enjoy your meals, and don't eat too fast. Try to make healthy eating a pleasure, not a chore.

Drink water instead of high-sugar drinks (including high-sugar juice drinks).

Junk or instant food gives you good taste and instant energy, but it affects your mood, concentration in studies and work, leads to many diseases.

Some more bad effects of non-veg foods:

- **It Might Contribute to Erectile Dysfunction in Men.**

Meat, eggs, and dairy products slow the flow of blood to all the body's organs — and not just the heart.

Originally, it was thought that impotence was caused only by anxiety, but according to the Erectile Dysfunction Institute, up to 90 percent of all cases of impotence are actually physical as opposed to psychological, meaning the high cholesterol, obesity, diabetes, prostate cancer or inflammations, and hormonal imbalances that eating meat causes might also contribute to impotence.

A new study published in The American Journal of Clinical Nutrition also suggests that men who couple regular exercise with a diet rich in flavonoids, which are found in fruits like strawberries, blueberries, and apples, may reduce their risk of developing Erectile Dysfunction by over 20 percent.

Numerous physicians and nutritionists agree that the best way to prevent artery blockage as well as multiple other conditions that because impotence is to eat a diet high in fiber, including plenty of fruits, vegetables, and whole grains. Of course, you can still eat these foods if you eat meat, but you're going to have fewer servings over time, and more health risks added into the mix.

- **Most Meat Has Hormones in It**

To make cows grow in an unnaturally fast rate, the cattle industry feeds them pellets full of hormones. While low levels of naturally occurring, hormones are found in various foods, many scientists are concerned that the artificial hormones injected into cows especially cause health problems in people who eat them. And while organic or hormone-free meat might be a better option, you're also not eliminating your chances of ingesting the naturally occurring sex hormones present in the animals when they were killed. The sex hormones progesterone, testosterone, and estrogen are all naturally occurring in animals, whether they've been given artificial hormones or not — so when you eat those animals, you're also eating hormones.

- **It May Make You Resistant to Antibiotics**

Factory farms are breeding grounds for antibiotic-resistant bacteria, known as "supergerms." On farms across America, the antibiotics that we depend on to treat human illnesses are now used to promote growth in animals and to keep them alive in horrific living conditions that would otherwise kill them. Countless new strains of antibiotic-resistant bacteria have developed as a result.

Roughly 70 percent of the antibiotics used in the United States each year are given to animals that are used for food, meaning if you eat meat, you run a greater risk of making yourself antibiotic-resistant. Vancomycin, a drug that is known as a "last defense" in fighting the deadly blood infections and pneumonia caused by staphylococcus bacteria, is becoming obsolete because resistant strains have developed in farmed animals who are given the medicine as a growth stimulant.

- **It Increases Your Risk of Death**

In large part because of all the health risks mentioned above, meat eaters just don't live if vegetarians and vegans. According to a study of over 70,000 people published in the journal JAMA Internal Medicine, vegetarians were 12 percent less likely to have died during a six-year follow up period than their meat-eating peers. Vegetarian men live to an average of 83.3 years, compared with non-vegetarian men, who live to an average of 73.8 years. Vegetarian women live to an average of 85.7 years, which is 6.1 years longer than non-vegetarian women, according to the Adventist Health Study-2. If you'd like to go the distance, looks like cutting out animals is one of the simplest things you can do.

The bottom line? One of the best things you can do for your health is to either eat less meat or cut it out altogether. Instead of contributing to the destruction of your body, the environment, and animals' lives, you'll be on the side of health, sustainability, and respect for all living beings.

Virat Kohli turned vegetarian and the run-machine is now on a new diet plan to further improve his fitness.

Tennis superstars Serena and Venus Williams, four-time Formula One champion Lewis Hamilton and legendary sprinter Carl Lewis are among the top athletes who turned vegetarian in the past.

Kohli is undoubtedly among the fittest athletes in the world and being the youth icon that he is, people look up to him. The India captain has been setting fitness goals not only for the masses but also for other professional athletes around the world.

Many famous personalities are/were vegetarians, many Scientist, Doctors, industrialist, sports players, actors and actresses, politicians, philosophers, philanthropist...

> ***"Let food be thy medicine and medicine be thy food."***
>
> **— Hippocrates**

CRITICISM, INSULT, BLAME

Three negative words which are detrimental when you are going up the ladder are, Criticism, Insult and Blame game. When you are on the path of success, some people won't like it and it is natural, they will criticize, put you down. This is the phase of life where many successful people can't handle themselves, they lose track out of frustration, negative pressure, fear of losing image.

Some people will always criticize you even if you do a right thing, even gods have not been spared by people and some people will praise even if someone does wrong activities. Terrorist and Naxalites also have their fan following.

> *"To avoid criticism, say nothing, do nothing, be nothing."*
>
> *- Elbert Hubbard*

So, don't give remote control of your life to someone, if someone is criticizing constructively, take their feedback positively to improve yourself. If the criticism is destructive, just have a strong will to ignore such criticism. Constructive criticism is always healthy with suggestions to improve and destructive criticism is always out of jealousy to put you down. People criticize most of the time to a person who is on the path of success, so be proud and take whatever good in feedback or just ignore if it is out of hate.

> *"Do not let arrogance go to your head and despair to your heart; do not let compliments go to your*

> ***head and criticisms to your heart; do not let success go to your head and failure to your heart."***
>
> ***— Roy T. Bennett, The Light in the Heart***

> ***"You can't progress unless you learn not only to receive criticism, but also invite criticism."***

Insult is another deeply hurting phenomenon affecting mental health and backtracks from the goal. Many times, due to highly stressful situation, someone insults you even though that person had no intention so just relax so don't take their words to your heart. Even if someone insults you out of jealousy, it is their frustration, so you don't have to accept it on mind level, just ignore and move ahead to achieve your goal, once you achieve everything falls in place.

When we come to know that whatever we are doing is not happening as per our wish, our mind tries to put blame on others. What happens, by blaming others, we close the doors to learn and improve ourselves from that activity/project/goal. Rather than blaming, act on the shortcomings in your actions, you will surely achieve sooner or later.

> ***"You don't have to disrespect and insult others simply to hold your ground, if you do, that shows how shaky is your own position is."***
>
> ***"Blaming others takes time and energy away from improving yourself."***
>
> ***Flaw laden intellect shows faults in others. If you deviate even slightly in the wrong direction, you will see everyone at fault.***

Param Pujya Dada Bhagwan

FAMOUS PERSONALITIES

One of the major reason why today's youths are confused, frustrated is that they are inspired by the wrong personalities. I do not blame them as nobody is interested to teach them or guide them about what to read, get inspired and follow in their life. Our education lacks these leaders on deeper level.

These personalities teach us how to lead a life in adverse situations, turn them into opportunities and come out as a winner. They show the world that commitment, passion, hard work, love for society and country, perseverance can take us on the path of success even though life looks difficult. I have given little window for you to go through few personalities, I would request everyone to read about these great warriors in depth, there are so many personalities which cannot be covered in this book but you should read about them. It will inspire everyone and will help to boost confidence in bad phase of life, at the same time, you will also learn that life is never smooth for anyone in life whether rich or poor, white or black.

Develop a habit of reading good material daily for few minutes. It will add new dimensions to your life which your never thought of.

Chhatrapati Shri Shivaji Maharaj

Chhatrapati Shivaji Maharaj was the founder of the Maratha Empire in western India. He is one of the greatest warriors of his time and even today, stories of his exploits are narrated as a part of the folklore. With his valor and great administrative skills, Shivaji carved out an enclave from the declining Adilshahi sultanate of Bijapur. It eventually became the genesis of the Maratha Empire. After establishing his rule, Shivaji implemented a competent and progressive administration with the help of a disciplined military and well-established administrative set-up. Shivaji is well-known for his innovative military tactics that centered around non-conventional methods leveraging strategic factors like geography, speed, and surprise to defeat his more powerful enemies.

Shivaji as an empire and nation builder:

Although several circumstances are said to be responsible for the rise of Shivaji and his building a strong nation and an empire, but the fact remains that it was his charismatic personality that was responsible for his phenomenal achievement.

Circumstances in fact already existed and no body tried to make use of these. It was Shivaji who took the initiative and shaped the circumstances according to his mold.

12 Major Qualities of Shivaji –

1. An effective organiser:

Shivaji is known as one of the greatest organizers in history.

By his remarkable powers, he collected the scattered Marathas and turned them into an organised formidable force.

2. *An efficient general and military strategist:*

He was a successful military general and knew well how to strike at the enemy. As a result of his strategies, he was able to face the mighty armies of the Sultans of Bijapur and the Mughals.

3. *A skillful diplomat:*

He never let his enemies unite against him. He got his father free from the Sultan of Bijapur on account of his diplomacy. His freedom from the detention of Aurangzeb at Agra speaks volumes of his diplomacy.

4. *Brave soldier:*

He was very daring and was prepared to take calculated risks.

5. *An enlightened administrator:*

Shivaji was an administrator of great ability and practical vision. He personally looked after the working of various departments. He was ruthless with those officers who indulged in corruption and oppression.

6. *Respect for others faith:*

His treatment with the followers of other faiths was very fair. Even a great critic of Shivaji like Khafi Khan has observed about him that he had "made it a rule that whenever his followers went plundering, they should do no harm to the mosques, the Book of God (Quran) or the women of anyone."

7. *An inspiring leader:*

His influence on account of his inspiring leadership grew so rapidly that his staunch enemy Aurangzeb himself had to admit "My armies have been employed against him for nineteen years and nevertheless his (Shivaji's) state has always been increasing."

8. *An obedient son:*

Shivaji loved his parents greatly. He was extremely devoted to his mother Jijabai. He worshipped her like a goddess and obeyed her command.

9. *A dutiful disciple:*

Shivaji had a great respect for his gurus.

10. *Regenerator of the Hindus:*

Shivaji attempted to generate a new spirit of pride among the Hindus. He, however, was also very particular to maintain the honor of Muslim women and the holy Quran.

11. *A benevolent ruler:*

Shivaji worked for the welfare of his subjects.

12. *Shivaji as the maker of Maharashtra:*

Shivaji welded the Maratha race into a mighty nation and he achieved all this in the teeth of the opposition of mighty powers like the Mughals, Bijapur and the Portuguese in India. As J.N. Sarkar, the great historian said, "He welded the Marathas into a mighty nation."

A benevolent administrator:

Dr. R.C. Majumdar writes of him, "He was not merely a daring soldier and successful military conqueror but also an enlightened ruler of his people." Shivaji was readily accessible to his all subjects. He was a popular monarch. He kept a close watch on the administrative affairs of the state. All powers were concentrated on him, but he ruled with the advice of his ministers. The common people regarded him with great devotion. They considered him as their greatest benefactor.

General features of Shivaji's administration:

1. He employed members of all castes and tribes to maintain balance among them.
2. He assigned separate responsibilities to the ministers and each of them was made responsible for his work to him.
3. He made no office hereditary.
4. In general, he did not assign jagirs to his civil and military officers.
5. He gave special attention towards the administration of the forts.
6. In matters of administration, he gave superior position to his civil officers as compared to military officers.
7. He established Ryotwari system in revenue administration. The state kept direct contact with the farmers.

Shivaji took special care to make his administrative system responsive to the needs of the people. In the words of Dr. Ishwari Prasad, "The institutions which he established were an improvement upon the existing order and were well adapted to the well-being of his subjects."

Central Administration:

He had a council of ministers (Asht Pradhari) to advise him on the matters of the state but he was not bound by it. He could appoint or dismiss them. This appointment was subject to their efficiency. The Peshwa was the first among ministers. The word Peshwa stands for leader or senior one.

Shivaji wrote a strong letter of protest to Aurangzeb. He wrote "God is the Lord of all men and not of the Muhammadans only. Islam and Hinduism are only different pigments used by the Divine Painter to picture the human species." At the same time Shivaji was never actuated by a hatred of the Muslims. He respected the personal honor of a Muslim.

Swami Vivekanand

Swami Vivekananda is a name that inspires admiration and awe around the globe. His words and teachings have influenced the greatest scientists like Nikol Tesla, visionaries like J.R.D Tata to several top leaders of the countries.

When he spoke in Chicago in the parliament of religions in 1891, the world took notice of his message of universal brotherhood. His extra ordinary life and mission changed the perspective of foreign countries towards the cultural superpower, named India.

Swami Vivekananda's teachings continue to inspire men to live their highest ideals and dedicate themselves to their highest pursuit. He was a leader who is reminisced by generations and continues to be a guiding force for leaders of the world.

Swami Vivekananda preached sacrifice, dedication, service and work with absolute commitment. He aroused the highest capabilities in a man by reminding them of their own divinity that made anything possible.

India celebrates his birthday as National Youth Day to celebrate the wisdom, teachings and mission of the soul that illumined the world with his presence. Here we look at the top leadership lessons from the timeless master.

7 Leadership Lessons From Swami Vivekananda

1. *Believe in Yourself*

Leadership lessons

> *"Believe in yourself and the world will be at your feet."*

A leader needs to believe in himself, his mission and what he is doing. When you have unwavering faith and belief, you find ways to accomplish things you want in your life. Difficulties, hardships and struggle make a true leader more determined to succeed.

2. Dedication to Work

Youth Day

> *"Even the greatest fool can accomplish a task if it were after his or her heart. But the intelligent ones are those who can convert every work into one that suits their taste."*

All great leaders remain deeply dedicated to his work. It doesn't matter what are you doing, but how you are doing it that makes the ultimate difference. Great opportunities are always possible for the one who is dedicated to what he is doing.

3. Face the Problem

Swami Vivekananda on Leadership

> *"If you ever feel afraid of anything, always turn around and face it. Never think of running away."*

A true leader will always have a mission and purpose in life. He will be ready to fight the world for it. You cannot solve problems by running away from them. Sooner or later, you will need to face the problems and conquer your fears. Leaders inspire people to face problems and find solutions for the benefit of all.

4. Focus on the goal

Universal Leadership

> *"Whatever you are doing, put your whole mind on it. If you are shooting, your mind should only be on*

> *the target. Then you will never miss. If you are learning your lessons, think only of the lesson."*

The difference in quality of two men lies in their ability to concentrate. When you focus your mind, energies and work towards your goals, success is assured. Leaders who work with single pointed focus are achieve their goals and vision.

5. Motivator

Great Leaders

> *"All power is within you. You can do anything and everything. Believe in that"*

Leaders empower their people by believing in them, trusting them and they rise to greatness as a result. A leader instills belief in others where they can accomplish things that they never thought were possible. Swami Vivekananda preached about the infinite power that resides in each of us and how it unleashes itself to help us achieve anything we want.

6. Strong Intentions and Resolutions

Strong Intentions

> *"There is no impossible word in the dictionary of those who lead. No matter how big a challenge, they can be resolved with strong intentions and resolutions."*

A leader always has great intentions, big vision and the resolution to try until he succeeds. When you are working on a noble mission with the right intentions, you may face hurdles, but you will make it in the end. Important is not to lose focus, change directions or give up.

Great efforts always lead to great results. Every problem is a challenge that can be overcome when you have a strong resolve.

7. *Stay Disciplined*

> *"Leader is one who knows how to obey commands before knowing how to command. Learn obedience first."*

A leader knows the rules of the game. He is the one who sets the benchmark for others to follow. Leaders take the responsibility; they walk the talk and never ask their teams to do what they wouldn't do themselves. A leader sets high expectations, standards and ideas for others to follow.

To sum up Swami Vivekananda's life and selfless leadership, he once said "This life is short, the vanities of the world are transient, but they alone live who live for others, the rest are more dead than alive."

Praveen Kumar Goudar, worked at Ramakrishna Mission (2009-2016)

Swami Vivekananda is a man of compassion and affection. He is a rare personality and boon to the world. He is a visionary of the world. His contribution to the people of India and the world in general is immeasurable. Swami Vivekananda is an extraordinary genius with both a spiritual vision and a spiritual mission. In his vision, man is none other than the supreme divinity under a tiny material cover, and human life is nothing but a continuous struggle to express that divinity within.

According to him, that society is the highest which affords maximum opportunities to its members to manifest their potential divinity. His mission, then, is to rouse men and women all over the world to an awareness of their divine nature and to show them the ways and means to express that divinity into their thought and actions—in their art, education, literature, culture, social customs and institutions, and, in fact, in all areas of life.

As Swami Vivekananda is a world teacher, his vision has encompassed the spiritual uplift of humanity, yet he is also one of the greatest leaders of modern India. He has tirelessly worked for India's regeneration, not only because he was born in India, but also because he has seen that her rich spiritual culture would be the greatest gift to world culture and civilization.

He has visualized that a spiritually awakened India would once again bring out a spiritualization of human life and culture in the world. His ideas and ideals have great relevance to the current problems challenging India and the world today. He is a rare and multi-faceted-nonpareil personality without any comparison. He is a prophet who has propagated the India's culture, Hindu Dharma, the secret of world peace, friendliness and equality.

Swami Vivekananda's speeches, lectures, poems and letters embody the emotional, intellectual and spiritual concerns of mankind. His condemnation of the exploiting tendency of the rich Indians and pity for the miserable condition of the poor brethren in his speeches and lectures, testify to his emotional concern. Hence in his speech: "To my brave boys" he makes an appeal: "Feel, my children, feel; feel for the poor, the ignorant, and the down-trodden; feel till the heart stops and the brain reels and you think you will go mad". Swami Vivekananda says that education is very much essential for the uplift of poor. Lack of education has made the poor to fall a prey to dogmatic ideas. He hits the nail on the head when he publicly diagnoses:

"The root of all evils in India is the condition of the poor. The poor in the West are devils; compared to them ours are angels, and it is therefore so much the easier to raise our poor. The only service to be done for our lower classes is to give them education, to develop their lost individuality. That is the great task between our people and the princes. Up to now nothing has been done in that direction. Priest-power and foreign conquest have trodden them down for centuries, and at last the poor of India have forgotten that they are human beings."

Dr. A P J Abdul Kalam

Dr. Avul Pakir Jainulabdeen Abdul Kalam born on 15th October 1931 at Rameswaram, in Tamil Nadu, specialized in Aero Engineering from Madras Institute of Technology.

Before his term as India's president, he worked as an aeronautical engineer with DRDO and ISRO. He is popularly known as the Missile Man of India for his work on development of ballistic missile and space rocket technology. In India he is highly respected as a scientist and as an engineer.

Kalam played a pivotal organisational, technical and political role in India's Pokhran-II nuclear test in 1998, the first since the original nuclear test by India in 1974. He was a professor at Anna University (Chennai) and adjunct/visiting faculty at many other academic and research institutions across India.

Political views

APJ Abdul Kalam views on certain issues have been espoused by him in his book India 2020 where he strongly advocates an action plan to develop India into a knowledge superpower and into a developed nation by the year 2020. Kalam is credited with the view that India ought to take a more assertive stance in international relations, he regards his work on India's nuclear weapons program to assert India's place as a future superpower.

Kalam continues to take an active interest in other developments in the field of science and technology as well. He has proposed a research programme for developing bio-implants. He is a supporter of Open source software over proprietary solutions and believes that the use of open source software on a large scale will bring more people the benefits of information technology...

Kalam's belief in the power of science to resolve society's problems and his views of these problems as a result of inefficient distribution of resources is modernistic. He also sees science and technology as ideology-free areas and emphasises the cultivation of scientific temper and entrepreneurial drive. In this, he finds a lot of support among India's new business leaders like the founders of Infosys and Wipro, (leading Indian IT corporations) who began their careers as technology professionals much in the same way Kalam did.

Personal life

Kalam's father was a devout Muslim, who owned boats which he rented out to local fishermen and was a good friend of Hindu religious leaders and the school - teachers at Rameshwaram. APJ Abdul Kalam mentions in his biography that to support his studies, he started his career as a newspaper vendor. This was also told in the book, A Boy and His Dream: Three Stories from the Childhood of Abdul Kalam by Vinita Krishna. The house Kalam was born in can still be found on the Mosque street in Rameshwaram, and his brother's curio shop abuts it. This has become a point-of-call for tourists who seek out the place.

Kalam grew up in an intimate relationship with nature, and he says in Wings of Fire that he never could imagine that water could be so powerful a destroying force as that he witnessed when he was thirty-three. That was in 1964 when a cyclonic storm swept away the Pamban bridge and a trainload of passengers with it and Kalam's native village, Dhanushkodi.

He is a scholar of Thirukkural, in most of his speeches, he quotes at least one kural. Kalam has written several inspirational books, most notably his autobiography Wings of Fire, aimed at motivating Indian youth. Another of his books, Guiding Souls: Dialogues on the Purpose of Life reveals his spiritual side. He has written poems in Tamil as well. It has been reported that there is considerable demand in South Korea for translated versions of books authored by him.

Kalam has also patronized grassroots innovations. He is closely associated with the Honeybee Network and The National innovation Foundation. The NIF is a body of Government of India and operates from Ahmadabad, Gujrat. He respects all religions, including Sikhism and Hinduism.

He is a vegetarian and a teetotaler.

Kalam as an engineer

Abdul Kalam graduated from Madras Institute of Technology majoring in Aeronautical Engineering. As the Project Director, he was heavily involved in the development of India's first indigenous Satellite Launch Vehicle (SLV-III). As Chief Executive of Integrated Guided Missile Development Programme (IGMDP), he also played a major part in developing many missiles of India including Agni and Prithvi. Although the entire project has been criticized for being overrun and mismanaged.

He was the Chief Scientific Adviser to Defense Minister and Secretary, Department of Defense Research & Development from July 1992 to December 1999.

Pokhran-II nuclear tests were conducted during this period, led by him.

He is one of those scientists who aims at putting technology created by him to multiple use. He used the light - weight carbon-compound material designed for Agni to make callipers for the polio affected. This carbon composite material reduced the weight of the calipers to 400 grams (from its original weight of 4kgs.) Nizam's Institute of Medical Sciences (NIMS, Hyderabad) was the birthplace for the defense technology spin offs from Kalam's labs via the DRDL (Defense Research and Development Laboratory), DMRL (Defense Metallurgical Research Lab) and the RCI (Research Centre Imarat). Addressing a conference at Athens, Greece, Kalam told that "Seeing the children run with lighter callipers brought tears to the eyes of their parents. That was the real moment of bliss for me".

Honours

On Wednesday April 29, 2009, he became the first Asian to be bestowed the Hoover Medal, America's top engineering prize, for his outstanding contribution to public service. Kalam has received honorary doctorates from as many as thirty universities, including the Carnegie Mellon University and the Nanyang Technological University of Singapore.

The Government of India, has honoured him with the nation's highest civilian honours: the Padma Bhushan in 1981; Padma Vibhushan in 1990; and the Bharat Ratna in 1997 for his work with ISRO and DRDO and his role as a scientific advisor to the Indian government...

Kalam is the Third President of India to have been honoured with a Bharat Ratna before being elected to the highest office, the other two being Sarvepalli Radhakrishnan and Zakir Hussain. He is also the first scientist and first bachelor to occupy Rashtrapati Bhavan.

Kalam has been chosen to receive prestigious 2008 Hoover Medal for his outstanding public service. The citation said that he is being recognised for making state-of-the-art healthcare available to the common man at affordable prices, bringing quality medical care to rural areas by establishing a link between doctors and technocrats, using spin-offs of defense technology to create state-of-the-art medical equipment and launching tele-medicine projects connecting remote rural-based hospitals to the super-specialty hospital. A pre - eminent scientist, a gifted engineer, and a true visionary, he is also a humble humanitarian in every sense of the word, it added.

Here are the 10 success lessons from APJ Abdul Kalam – "Missile Man of India" for entrepreneurs

1. *Be a leader*

He inspired leaderships by example. During 1980s, he was able to convince Indira Gandhi, then Prime Minister of India, to allocate funds for aerospace projects under his directorship, despite the Union Cabinet's disapproval. These projects were instrumental in the growth of India's space research program.

"Let me define a leader. He must have vision and passion and not be afraid of any problem. Instead, he should know how to defeat it. Most importantly, he must work with integrity."

Indeed, his last words were about the qualities that constituted a great leader.

2. Be a dreamer

Under Dr. Kalam's leadership, a budget of INR 388 crores was sanctioned for the Integrated Guided Missile Development Program (IGMDP) by the Union Government. The program started in 1982-83 and lasted 15 years.

After India test fired Prithvi in 1988 and Agni in 1989, under this program, many countries restricted access to any technology that would help India with its missile program. Undaunted, Kalam carried on with the dream program and this pushed India to successfully develop critical technology, indigenously. True entrepreneurs dream big and then work towards turning their dreams into reality. "You have to dream before your dreams can come true."

3. Push the boundaries

As a young student at MIT, Kalam was told by his professor to recreate an aircraft design from the scratch or lose his scholarship. Moreover, he was given only 3 days to finish a job which ideally would have taken weeks. With sheer determination, he came up with a design that won him accolades from the same professor.

Entrepreneurs face seemingly uphill tasks with strict deadlines in a "succeed or perish" environment. The key is to apply oneself and work towards a solution. "There is no such thing as an impossible deadline".

4. Take responsibility

During one of the test flights, for an underdevelopment aircraft surveillance system, a plane crash killed the entire crew of 8 men. That day Dr. Kalam felt the weight of being responsible for someone else.

As entrepreneurs, we lead teams. Leading teams can be challenging. Much more challenging can be sharing success and taking responsibility for failure. "Don't pretend to be a candle, be a moth. Know the power hidden in serving."

5. *Defeat the problem and succeed!*

"If you're on a new mission or a complex task, you should also expect to experience equally challenging problems. You should not allow the problem to become your captain. You should become the captain of the problem, defeat the problem and succeed."

These were the words Abdul Kalam's professor gave him once and he's followed them throughout his life and is also what he suggests to young entrepreneurs. "This may be true for every one of you in the decision making process, venture capital acquisition, equipment procurement, commissioning equipment, paying back large loans, acquisition of human resource, training of human resource, marketing of your products and every one of your day-to-day activities as an entrepreneur.

6. *Keep fit*

Successful people realize the importance of a healthy body and a healthy mind. They know that the two are inextricably inter-linked and imperative for their smooth functioning. They follow a strict regime of healthy habits which include right eating, adherence to mealtimes, a holistic exercise plan that suits one's age and a mind full of positivity. It is established that the first three invariably impact the fourth.

7. *Be tenacious*

After his longstanding dream of becoming a pilot with India Air Force got shattered, young Kalam got his act together and accepted an opportunity with the Ministry of Defense. He convinced himself that much better opportunities lay ahead. In his words, "Man needs difficulties in life because they are necessary to enjoy the success".

8. *Think different*

Kalam never believed in doing a run-of-the-mill job and encouraged others to do things differently, especially the younger generation. He believed that entrepreneurship should be included as a course in India's, which is otherwise a rote-learning based educational system.

He once said, "My message, especially to young people is to have courage to think differently, courage to invent, to travel the unexplored path, courage to discover the impossible and to conquer the problems and succeed. These are great qualities that they must work towards. This is my message to the young people."

9. *Connect with people*

In the mad race for success, we often distance people and embrace numbers. If this is inadvertent and not deliberate, the realization of the same comes as a shock to even oneself. Gregarious that we are by nature, it is in our best interest that we try to know our neighbors/surroundings and keep in touch with our family. This also helps in self-introspection of oneself.

10. *Work hard*

Even during his last day, Dr. Kalam never stepped back an inch to deliver that speech. "The whole universe is friendly to us and conspires only to give the best to those who dream and work." This saying shows how Dr. Kalam used to define the day by working hard.

Steve Jobs

American business executive, computer programmer, and entrepreneur

Computer designer and corporate executive Steve Jobs is cofounder of Apple Computers. With his vision of affordable personal computers, he launched one of the largest industries of the past decades while still in his early twenties. He remains one of the most inventive and energetic minds in American technology.

Early life

Steven Jobs was born February 24, 1955, in San Francisco, California, and was adopted by Paul and Clara Jobs. He grew up with one sister, Patty. Paul Jobs was a machinist and fixed cars as a hobby. Jobs remembers his father as being very skilled at working with his hands.

In 1961 the family moved to Mountain View, California. This area, just south of Palo Alto, California, was becoming a center for electronics. Electronics form the basic elements of devices such as radios, televisions, stereos, and computers. At that time people started to refer to the area as "Silicon Valley." This is because a substance called silicon is used in the manufacturing of electronic parts.

As a child, Jobs preferred doing things by himself. He swam competitively but was not interested in team sports or other group activities. He showed an early interest in electronics and gadgetry. He spent a lot of time working in the garage workshop of a neighbor who worked at Hewlett-Packard, an electronics manufacturer.

Jobs also enrolled in the Hewlett-Packard Explorer Club. There he saw engineers demonstrate new products, and he saw his first computer at the age of twelve. He was very impressed and knew right away that he wanted to work with computers.

While in high school Jobs attended lectures at the Hewlett-Packard plant. On one occasion he boldly asked William Hewlett (1931–2001), the president, for some parts he needed to complete a class project. Hewlett was so impressed he gave Jobs the parts and offered him a summer internship at Hewlett-Packard.

Here are the top 10 Steve Jobs rules for success.

1. Don't live a limited life

"Your time is limited, so don't waste it living someone else's life. Don't be trapped by dogma – which is living with the results of other people's thinking. Don't let the noise of other's opinions drown out your own inner voice. And most important, have the courage to follow your heart and intuition. They somehow already know what you truly want to become. Everything else is secondary." – Steve Jobs

2. Have passion

If you're not passionate enough from the start, you'll never stick it out. With any job, there are aspects of work that are frustrating and difficult—even with the greatest dream job in the world but being passionate about it will make you able to hold on when things get rough.

3. Design for yourself

"Don't let the noise of others' opinions drown out your own inner voice." – Steve Jobs

I know it's cliché, but this is so true, you are the captain of your own ship; don't let anyone else take the wheel. Design life for yourself, you won't receive a second opportunity to do so, so you either do it now, or you regret it on later in life.

4. *Don't sell crap*

Sell only high-quality products, while many would argue I would say that Apple products have always been top quality and that's the reason why they are still at the top. They just provide quality products, and because of that they have loyal customers that are always willing to buy.

5. *Build a great team*

The people you surround yourself with, are the people that will shape your future. If you surround yourself with smart and positive people that share your vision, well then, you have a bright future ahead of you. Remember that you are the average of the five people you spend the most time with, so choose wisely.

6. *Don't do it for the money*

Choose a job you love, and you will never have to work a day in your life. Steve Jobs was worth 100 million dollars when he was 25 years old, but he didn't do it for the money. He did it because he wanted to change the world, he was an innovator.

7. *Be proud of your products*

Create products that you can proudly recommend to friends and family, if your product is great, money will follow. Make sure your product is high quality and it's something that people would love to use.

8. *__Build around customers__*

Customers tend to trust individuals who are serious about what they do, and willing to take the time to achieve a deep understanding of their craft. Take the time every day to learn more about your customers, their industry and their challenges.

Gaining trust is only part of the equation. You must also have a product that customers want and need, and the ability to show how you're adding value, solving problems, and so forth. However, if you don't earn the customer's trust, they'll probably buy from someone else whom they do trust–even if the offering isn't as good.

9.   *Marketing is about Values*

Have you ever seen a Nike advertisement where they share why they are better than Adidas and Puma? No, I know you haven't, because what they do is, they honor great athletes like Michael Jordan – that's what they are, that's who they are. So, make sure your customers know what your company stands for.

10. *Stay Hungry, Stay Foolish*

Never be satisfied, and always push yourself. Do (or be willing to keep trying) the things people say cannot be done.

Top 10 Achievements Of Steve Jobs

1.   *Igniting the personal computer revolution.*

With the Apple II and the Macintosh, Jobs and the then-named Apple Computer (AAPL) helped to launch the PC revolution. The Apple II, released in 1977, was one of the first highly successful mass-produced personal computers. The Macintosh, introduced in 1984, was the first commercially successful PC to use a mouse and graphical user interface.

2.   *Introducing the mouse and graphical user interface.*

Jobs changed how people interact with personal computers by replacing the text-based command-line interface with a mouse-driven graphical user interface. Instead of typing in commands with a keyboard, users could click on on-screen icons using a mouse controller. Jobs borrowed the idea for the new interface from Xerox 's (XRX) Palo Alto Research Center, which failed to see its potential.

3. *Bringing portable music players to the masses.*

Others had come out with portable digital music players before Apple debuted the iPod in 2001. But Apple made the device a fun, simple and fashionable way to store thousands of songs. Jobs' creation soon dominated the market.

4. *Revolutionizing the sale of music.*

Jobs turned music distribution on its head with the iTunes store by offering consumers an easy and affordable way to download songs to their computers and iPods. The iTunes store offered people an alternative to buying music CDs or illegally downloading songs from online sharing services.

5. *Shepherding the age of computer animation.*

Jobs ushered in the age of feature-length computer-animated movies by funding and leading Pixar Animation Studios. Jobs bought an unproven animation studio from George Lucas in 1986 and turned it into a maker of blockbuster films, starting with "Toy Story" in 1995. Walt Disney (DIS) purchased Pixar in 2006 for $7.4 billion.

6. *Opening Apple stores.*

Jobs defied the skeptics when he launched a chain of Apple retail stores starting in 2001. The stores have proved to be a huge success, not only in selling products but also extending the Apple brand and cachet worldwide. Apple now operates more than 350 stores.

7. *Making personal computers stylish.*

From the start, Apple computers have stood out as stylish. From the candy-colored original iMacs to the super thin MacBook Air, Apple has made products that consumers crave. When it came to Apple's products, Jobs sweated the details of fit and finish.

8. *Launching the smartphone revolution.*

When Jobs got Apple into the mobile phone business with the iPhone in 2007, he didn't just add cellular phone capabilities to an iPod or vice versa, as some expected. He came out with a landmark device that merged an iPod, full Internet browser and mobile phone into a beautiful gadget with a multitouch-screen interface. The iPhone was an instant hit and begat a thousand copycats.

9. *Changing how software applications are distributed.*

Jobs changed how software applications are distributed when he opened the App Store for downloading applications to the iPhone and iPod Touch in 2008. He gave developers a way to write and sell mobile programs to consumers online. Its success created a vibrant ecosystem that has boosted demand for Apple's mobile devices.

10. *Kicking off the tablet trend.*

Apple faced a lot of doubters when Jobs debuted the iPad tablet in April 2010. But the media tablet soon became another hit product.

Ratan Tata

If there is one name that stands out for trust and integrity, it's Ratan Tata. Born on 28 December 1937 in Surat, Ratan Naval Tata was the chairman of Tata Group, the Mumbai-based conglomerate from 1991–2012.

He has been awarded Padma Vibhushan and Padma Bhushan in the year 2008 & 2000 respectively for his contribution towards trade and industry. Known for his vision and ability to lead and innovate, he led the global foray of the largely India-based Tata Group. The 78-year-old began his career with the Tata Group in 1961, and spearheaded the company from a $1.5 billion market cap to a $100 billion market cap. The legendary scion has been an inspiration for leaders across the world.

Shri Ratan Tata

Ratan Tata is one of the leading Indian industrialists, ex-Chairman of the largest Indian conglomerate, Tata Group of Companies. He currently holds the post of Chairman Emeritus of Tata Sons, the holding company of the Tata Group which controls some of the major companies including Tata Steel, Tata Motors, Tata Power, Tata Consultancy Services, Indian Hotels and Tata Teleservices. Brought up by his grandmother from the age of ten when his parents separated, he became actively involved in the family business after completing his graduation. He started as a fellow worker on the shop floor at Tata Steel and gained an insight about his family business. After the retirement of J.R.D. Tata, he became the new Chairman of the Tata Group. Under his leadership, the organization achieved new heights and generated large amount of overseas revenues. He was instrumental in the acquisition of Tetley, Jaguar Land Rover and Corus, which turned Tata from a major India-Centric company to a global brand name. Apart from expanding his multinational, he has also served in various capacities in organizations in India and abroad. He is also a leading philanthropist and more than half of his share in the group is invested in charitable trusts. Through his pioneering ideas and positive outlook, he continues to serve as a guiding force for his conglomerate even after retirement.

Childhood & Early Life

He was born on December 28, 1937 in Surat, India, to Naval Tata and Sonoo. Naval Tata was the adopted son of the Jamsetji Tata's younger son Ratanji Tata. Jamsetji Tata was the founder of the Tata Group of Companies. Ratan Tata has a brother, Jimmy, and a step - brother, Noel Tata.

When he was ten, his parents, got separated and thereafter, he and his brother were brought up by his grandmother, Navajbai Tata.

He received his early education from the Campion School, Mumbai and finished his schooling from the Cathedral and John Connon School, Mumbai. In 1962, he obtained his B.S. in architecture with structural engineering from Cornell University, U.S.A.

Later he got enrolled at the Harvard Business School and completed an Advanced Management Program in 1975.

Here are the 10 Success lessons from Ratan Tata for entrepreneurs

1. Be a visionary

When Ratan Tata joined the group, it was barely doing any business outside India. Even though many opposed him, he maintained that the company had to go global. Today half of Tata's revenues come from overseas. Under his leadership Tata acquired brands like Tetley, Jaguar Land Rover, and Taj Boston.

2.   *Be humble*

He is known for his humility, and there are countless examples. He started out working as a blue-collar employee for Tata Steel. He personally visited the families of the 80 employees who were affected because of the 26/11 attacks. He remembers almost everyone by their first names and is not dismissive.

3.   *Never give up on values*

Values are something that define a company, both to its employees and its customers. Public Safety and welfare have always been one of the main core values of Tata. The Tata Group has always been known for upholding these values and when Ratan Tata took the reigns, he too reinstated these values into the company culture. As a result, Tata has become one of the most trusted brands the world over.

4.   *Take Risks*

Taking risks is the cardinal rule of business. As a leader, one needs to have the foresight and the capability to take risks that can take the company to new heights. Coming from business family, Ratan Tata was no stranger to taking risks and once also said, "I don't believe in making right decisions. I take decisions and then make them right." From acquiring the Jaguar and Land Rover businesses from Ford to taking over Corus, the second-largest steel maker in Europe, Ratan Tata made significantly big moves and has managed to make things work in his favour.

5. *Motivate others*

Ratan Tata had the ability to inspire and motivate others which is very important for a leader. Being a great leader isn't about checking all the right boxes but is about making sure you inspire, drive and spark your drive-in others, so that they along with you, can bring about change, social innovation and progress.

6. *Have faith in yourself*

When you are dealing with life's hodgepodge, every minute you take a decision. Some decisions are right while there are some decisions that may cause situations to take an unpredicted turn. At such junctures, before people lose faith in your decision-making skills, you must have staunch belief in yourself and must confidently come forward to make the situation in your favor.

7. *Be open to criticism*

As per a famous quote by Ratan Tata, 'Take the stones people throw at you and use them to build a monument.' Whenever you endeavor to do something you like, you won't always receive appreciation. There will be people who will try to pull you down and criticize to shatter your spirit. All you need to do is just ignore all the criticisms and focus on your work.

8. *Use creative tendencies*

Be creative rather than being reactive. Being proactive and solving problems even before they come is one of the most important qualities of an entrepreneur. A person should not tend to react only when the situation demands but the person should be able to be anticipate what will happen in future and be able to adjust himself to it in present. An entrepreneur who exercises such quality is always successful.

9. *Get out of the safe mode*

To be successful in business you need to take risk. No risk no gain. Mr. Ratan Tata always believed in taking risk and the result is clear that the risk paid off. To be successful you need to take risk working in safe mode might make you feel comfortable, but you will never be able to get best out of the system. He once said "I don't believe in making right decisions. I take decisions and then make them right,"

10. *Don't put all your eggs in one basket*

Mr. Ratan Tata believed in investing in different companies so as his investment is always safe. He acquired a stake in the growing Chinese giant Xiaomi and leading e-commerce site snapdeal. Investing in different companies ensures that your investment is safe and grows no what the situation of an industry is.

Pele

By Bree from San Diego

"Success is no accident. It is hard work, perseverance, learning, studying, sacrifice and most of all, love of what you are doing or learning to do." Pele. These words were said by the great Edson Arantes do Nascimento, or more commonly known as Pele. He was born on October 23, 1940 in Tres Coracoes, Brazil and he is still alive to this day.

Although his popular nickname was Pele, he acquired another nickname, the Perola Negra, or "Black Pearl" by some of his compatriots. Pele had dropped out of school by the age of nine and his father, Joao Ramos do Nascomento provided instructions on what he knew about soccer because he was a former minor league center forward for a Brazilian Soccer Club.

I doubt his father ever imagined his son would be such an extraordinary soccer player that changed the sport so immensely. Ever since he was a young boy, Pele's aspiration in life was to be a professional soccer player. Having grown up in poverty, realistically, his hopes might be inadequate.

Pele was not just another ordinary soccer player; he was an undeniable hero. This is partially because his bravery and mental toughness through the hardships he experienced. It was also due to the way he recreated soccer through his dedication, devotion, and heart he put into what he loved, shining and inspiring to others.

Pele grew up with a deficit and knew what it felt like to have to have the vigor through complications life presented him with and was accomplished in life because of his tough mentality and fortitude. For reference, Pele was more of a "street" player because of his poverty as shown, "Since he was quite poor, he could not afford to join some expensive club to learn football…Pele could not afford to buy a football, so, he used to practice with either a grapefruit or sock stuffed with newspaper tied with a string."("Pele Biography) Even through such a harsh environment, Pele's main focus was on enhancing his soccer skills, which shows his tenacity as he accomplished his objective.

Obviously, this was not a temperate task given his environment, so this demonstrates how determined he must have been with how little he had to improve with as a soccer player. In addition, Pele was seen as the stand-out player on the field arousing difficult as stated, "Injuries kept Pele out of Brazil's second World Cup win in 1962, but he led Santos to victories against Europe's top teams in the Copa Libertadores and the Intercontinental Cup in 1962 and 1963. But as Pele's reputation grew, so did infighting on the international soccer circuit. The Santos club's opponents focused all their efforts on injuring Pele, the mainstay of the team." ("Pelé." Discovering) Pele's daring ways shows he understands that he was the main target of the other team and he would always be risking injuries out on the field playing.

How is it that Pele handled all this pressure? He did have irritation and grievance towards the teams that purposely directed all their players to put him in such distress, but Pele was so courageous that he pushed past his discomfort for his love for the game. Undoubtedly, Pele had his fair share of struggles, but used his prowess to push beyond the contention on and off the field.

Pele was also very dedicated, devoted, and a passionate player, and it showed as his skill on the field took soccer to a whole new level stunning his viewers. This is evident in the statement, "By the time he was thirteen, Pele had captured the attention of World Cup great Waldemar de Brito, manager of Bauru junior team, Pele became one of the club's best players." ("Pelé." U*X*L) This shows how much effort and discipline Pele put into improving because of his zealous desire to grow as a soccer player. I could not imagine the massive amount of work he must have put in to have been recognized by a high-level coach at such a young age.

In addition, Pele can be summarized as, "A forward, Pele electrified crowds with his daring dribbling, perfect passing, and accurate shooting. He holds every major scoring record in Brazil and scored 1,281 goals in 1,363 games during his professional career. Pele is the only professional soccer player to score 1,000 goals in a career." ("Pele Biography) What an arduous achievement. It's unbelievable to really grasp the thought of how successful Pele really was. His love for the sport is obvious as he played 1,363 games, but you also can see how far his commitment got him and how much fanfare he brought to soccer.

We should give recognition for his accomplishments because he forever changed soccer as a spectator's sport. Pele was so comfortable and knowledgeable of the game and of the ball itself, that he knew when it was essential to take certain risks when he had possession. This contributed to the evolution and new understandings strategies of the game. In summary, Pele's loyalty and passion drove his skill to such an elevated level and made a lasting impact on the future of soccer.

His skill, devotion, mental toughness, and knowledge of the game are all qualities of Pele. Above all though, it is his true love for the game that makes Edson Arantes my hero and inspiration. I started my essay off with a quote from Pele himself because I feel that it defines him perfectly. That's just what Pele did. He learned to do what he loved the most to the best of his ability, so that he would not only enjoy what he was doing but be successful at it as well.

He describes the hard work and sacrifice it will take so we understand it will not be easy, yet we are still inspired. This is because Pele proved it possible. At such a young age he had set a goal to become a professional soccer player and he did that and much more. He arouses a sense of motivation as explained, "I saw Pele a few times afterward, when he was playing for the New York Cosmos. He was no longer as fast, but he was as exuberant as ever.

By then, Pele had become an institution. Most modern fans never saw him play, yet they somehow felt he was part of their lives. He made the transition from superstar to mythic figure." ("Pele Biography) Moreover, Time also explains him as, "Heroes walk alone, but they become myths when they ennoble the lives and touch the hearts of all of us. For those who love soccer, Edson Arantes do Nascimento, generally known as Pele, is a hero."("Pele Biography) Pele brought something new and special to the game, grasping the attention of youth soccer players largely because of the popularity he brought to the game. As you can see, because of Pele's determination, bravery, and passion he has changed soccer forever, and I can proudly say that he is part of my life as not only my inspiration, but my hero.

Nelson Mandela

Hearing the elders' stories of his ancestors' valour during the wars of resistance, he dreamed also of making his own contribution to the freedom struggle of his people.

He completed his BA through the University of South Africa and went back to Fort Hare for his graduation in 1943. Meanwhile, he began studying for an LLB at the University of the Witwatersrand. By his own admission he was a poor student and left the university in 1952 without graduating. He only started studying again through the University of London after his imprisonment in 1962 but also did not complete that degree.

In 1989, while in the last months of his imprisonment, he obtained an LLB through the University of South Africa.

Entering politics

Mandela, while increasingly politically involved from 1942, only joined the African National Congress in 1944 when he helped to form the ANC Youth League (ANCYL).

In 1944 he married Walter Sisulu's cousin, Evelyn Mase, a nurse. They had two sons, Madiba Thembekile "Thembi" and Makgatho, and two daughters both called Makaziwe, the first of whom died in infancy. He and his wife divorced in 1958.

Mandela rose through the ranks of the ANCYL and through its efforts, the ANC adopted a more radical mass-based policy, the Programme of Action, in 1949.

In 1952 he was chosen as the National Volunteer-in-Chief of the Defiance Campaign with Maulvi Cachalia as his deputy. This campaign of civil disobedience against six unjust laws was a joint programme between the ANC and the South African Indian Congress. He and 19 others were charged under the Suppression of Communism Act for their part in the campaign and sentenced to nine months of hard labor, suspended for two years.

A two-year diploma in law on top of his BA allowed Mandela to practice law, and in August 1952 he and Oliver Tambo established South Africa's first black law firm, Mandela & Tambo.

At the end of 1952 he was banned for the first time. As a restricted person he was only permitted to watch in secret as the Freedom Charter was adopted in Kliptown on 26 June 1955.

The Treason Trial

Mandela was arrested in a countrywide police swoop on 5 December 1956, which led to the 1956 Treason Trial. Men and women of all races found themselves in the dock in the marathon trial that only ended when the last 28 accused, including Mandela, were acquitted on 29 March 1961.

On 21 March 1960 police killed 69 unarmed people in a protest in Sharpeville against the pass laws. This led to the country's first state of emergency and the banning of the ANC and the Pan Africanist Congress (PAC) on 8 April. Mandela and his colleagues in the Treason Trial were among thousands detained during the state of emergency.

Days before the end of the Treason Trial, Mandela travelled to Pietermaritzburg to speak at the All-in Africa Conference, which resolved that he should write to Prime Minister Verwoerd requesting a national convention on a non-racial constitution, and to warn that should he not agree there would be a national strike against South Africa becoming a republic. After he and his colleagues were acquitted in the Treason Trial, Mandela went underground and began planning a national strike for 29, 30 and 31 March.

In the face of massive mobilization of state security, the strike was called off early. In June 1961 he was asked to lead the armed struggle and helped to establish Umkhonto we Sizwe (Spear of the Nation), which launched on 16 December 1961 with a series of explosions.

"I have fought against white domination, and I have fought against black domination. I have cherished the ideal of a democratic and free society in which all persons live together in harmony and with equal opportunities. It is an ideal which I hope to live for and to achieve. But if needs be, it is an ideal for which I am prepared to die."

Speech from the Dock quote by Nelson Mandela on 20 April 1964

On 11 June 1964 Mandela and seven other accused, Walter Sisulu, Ahmed Kathrada, Govan Mbeki, Raymond Mhlaba, Denis Goldberg, Elias Motsoaledi and Andrew Mlangeni, were convicted and the next day were sentenced to life imprisonment. Goldberg was sent to Pretoria Prison because he was white, while the others went to Robben Island.

Mandela's mother died in 1968 and his eldest son, Thembi, in 1969. He was not allowed to attend their funerals.

On 31 March 1982 Mandela was transferred to Pollsmoor Prison in Cape Town with Sisulu, Mhlaba and Mlangeni. Kathrada joined them in October. When he returned to the prison in November 1985 after prostate surgery, Mandela was held alone. Justice Minister Kobie Coetsee visited him in hospital. Later Mandela initiated talks about an ultimate meeting between the apartheid government and the ANC.

Release from prison

On 12 August 1988 he was taken to hospital where he was diagnosed with tuberculosis. After more than three months in two hospitals he was transferred on 7 December 1988 to a house at Victor Verster Prison near Paarl where he spent his last 14 months of imprisonment. He was released from its gates on Sunday 11 February 1990, nine days after the unbanning of the ANC and the PAC and nearly four months after the release of his remaining Rivonia comrades. Throughout his imprisonment he had rejected at least three conditional offers of release.

Mandela immersed himself in official talks to end white minority rule and in 1991 was elected ANC President to replace his ailing friend, Oliver Tambo. In 1993 he and President FW de Klerk jointly won the Nobel Peace Prize and on 27 April 1994 he voted for the first time in his life.

President

On 10 May 1994 he was inaugurated as South Africa's first democratically elected President. On his 80th birthday in 1998 he married Graça Machel, his third wife.

True to his promise, Mandela stepped down in 1999 after one term as President. He continued to work with the Nelson Mandela Children's Fund he set up in 1995 and established the Nelson Mandela Foundation and The Mandela Rhodes Foundation.

In April 2007 his grandson, Mandla Mandela, was installed as head of the Mvezo Traditional Council at a ceremony at the Mvezo Great Place.

Nelson Mandela never wavered in his devotion to democracy, equality and learning. Despite terrible provocation, he never answered racism with racism. His life is an inspiration to all who are oppressed and deprived; and to all who are opposed to oppression and deprivation.

He died at his home in Johannesburg on 5 December 2013.

Thomas Edison

Thomas Alva Edison was born on February 11, 1847 in Milan, Ohio; the seventh and last child of Samuel and Nancy Edison. When Edison was seven his family moved to Port Huron, Michigan. Edison lived here until he struck out on his own at the age of sixteen. Edison had very little formal education as a child, attending school only for a few months. He was taught reading, writing, and arithmetic by his mother, but was always a very curious child and taught himself much by reading on his own. This belief in self-improvement remained throughout his life.

Edison began working at an early age, as most boys did at the time. At thirteen he took a job as a newsboy, selling newspapers and candy on the local railroad that ran through Port Huron to Detroit. He seems to have spent much of his free time reading scientific, and technical books, and had the opportunity at this time to learn how to operate a telegraph. By the time he was sixteen, Edison was proficient enough to work as a telegrapher full time.

The first great invention developed by Edison in Menlo Park was the tin foil phonograph. The first machine that could record and reproduce sound created a sensation and brought Edison international fame. Edison toured the country with the tin foil phonograph and was invited to the White House to demonstrate it to President Rutherford B. Hayes in April 1878.

Edison next undertook his greatest challenge, the development of a practical incandescent, electric light. The idea of electric lighting was not new, and several people had worked on, and even developed forms of electric lighting. But up to that time, nothing had been developed that was remotely practical for home use. Edison's eventual achievement was inventing not just an incandescent electric light, but also an electric lighting system that contained all the elements necessary to make the incandescent light practical, safe, and economical.

After one and a half years of work, success was achieved when an incandescent lamp with a filament of carbonized sewing thread burned for thirteen and a half hours. The first public demonstration of the Edison's incandescent lighting system was in December 1879, when the Menlo Park laboratory complex was electrically lighted. Edison spent the next several years creating the electric industry. In September 1882, the first commercial power station, located on Pearl Street in lower Manhattan, went into operation providing light and power to customers in a one square mile area; the electric age had begun.

The success of his electric light brought Edison to new heights of fame and wealth, as electricity spread around the world. Edison's various electric companies continued to grow until in 1889 they were brought together to form Edison General Electric. Despite the use of Edison in the company title however, Edison never controlled this company. The tremendous amount of capital needed to develop the incandescent lighting industry had necessitated the involvement of investment bankers such as J.P. Morgan. When Edison General Electric merged with its leading competitor Thompson-Houston in 1892, Edison was dropped from the name, and the company became simply General Electric.

This period of success was marred by the death of Edison's wife Mary in 1884. Edison's involvement in the business end of the electric industry had caused Edison to spend less time in Menlo Park. After Mary's death, Edison was there even less, living instead in New York

City with his three children. A year later, while vacationing at a friend's house in New England, Edison met Mina Miller and fell in love. The couple was married in February 1886 and moved to West Orange, New Jersey where Edison had purchased an estate, Glenmont, for his bride. Thomas Edison lived here with Mina until his death.

When Edison moved to West Orange, he was doing experimental work in makeshift facilities in his electric lamp factory in nearby Harrison, New Jersey. A few months after his marriage, however, Edison decided to build a new laboratory in West Orange itself, less than a mile from his home. Edison possessed both the resources and experience by this time to build, "the best equipped and largest laboratory extant and the facilities superior to any other for rapid and cheap development of an invention ". The new laboratory complex consisting of five buildings opened in November 1887.

A three-story main laboratory building contained a power plant, machine shops, stock rooms, experimental rooms and a large library. Four smaller one-story buildings built perpendicular to the main building contained a physics lab, chemistry lab, metallurgy lab, pattern shop, and chemical storage. The large size of the laboratory not only allowed Edison to work on any sort of project, but also allowed him to work on as many as ten or twenty projects at once. Facilities were added to the laboratory or modified to meet Edison's changing needs as he continued to work in this complex until his death in 1931. Over the years, factories to manufacture Edison inventions were built around the laboratory. The entire laboratory and factory complex eventually covered more than twenty acres and employed 10,000 people at its peak during World War One (1914-1918).

VIEWPOINTS OF YOUTHS

When we give space to our youngsters to express, see how they express which is beyond our imagination. It was difficult for most of us to express the same when we were of their age. It is our duty and priority to have a balanced approach while handling them. It's like controlling the horse while riding. If you keep lose rein, horse will be out of control and if you hold it too tight, will be difficult for to move, leads to violence. Same think is applicable in our life, don't be too strict or too much lenient, Balancing is necessary.

Ameya Manoj Satpute

Engineering

What I feel personally…….

As a youth, many things are expected from us by the society, nation and even by our family. But getting a chance to express, what the youth expects is a rare opportunity to get. We always listen what people saying 'My child has lived up to my expectation", but nobody asks the child whether he has lived up to his own expectation or not. This is my major concern that I want to express in this writeup.

Yes, indeed Indian culture, Indian society has a very rich history. Our traditions and practices all have their own significance and importance and it should be carried on this way. But mindset of our society needs to be changed. We have always been taught, 'always listen to our elders', but nobody accepts that sometimes elders can also go wrong. The reason, I am saying this is because we are always told or forced to do a certain thing in a certain way. This is making today's generation a 'do as told' generation. We are losing our creativity. From school days we are taught a lesson, then we are given question-answers and then we mug up it and pour it all on a piece of paper called exam answer sheet; and all this process is summed up and evaluated in another piece of paper called report card. I am not saying this is wrong, but it could be better. This type of education system goes up till graduation and post-graduation and then we complain that today's generation is ineligible for industry and other outer world needs. But nobody sees that we have been only taught to compete with our classmates based on system called, 'who can mug up better'.

Ultimately, this led us to engineering projects having lack of innovation. Unfeasible solutions to real world problems and very small amount of new brilliant notions. What I want as youth is to make this upcoming generation a better decision maker, a better out of the box thinker, a better real-world problem solver. This could start just by making small changes in curriculum at school level. By adding selective subjects in the curriculum. Just to choose from multiple subjects in decision making process. This will allow the students to choose something of his own interest and allow his mind to start thinking in a different direction. Those subjects could be a full-time art topic design to appreciate artistry or a sports physics subject or a finance related topic any thing that makes a student's mind more inclusive and gives him or her a break from regular studies. Such small change can do long term effect.

Coming to higher education system we need more opportunities from ground zero. As an engineering student I spend my three months writing assignments, 1 month preparing for viva and practical and 1 month for semester exams. This gives me less time to learn the engineering because only learning theory in college will not make me an engineer. I want ample amount of time to process the theory and understand its real-world implications, instead of writing assignments based on that theory. Luckily, I have guides to help me to through this practicality parts but among other students there are brilliant engineers, but they lack the application knowledge and thus as a nation we lagging behind.

We have not lived as per our expected grown - ups' version, we wanted to be in our childhood but yes for once listening to youth and making certain changes can change the whole scenario. I am not an expert in this field but if these changes were made available to me and my friends, we would definitely be in much better position than what we are today.

Swapnil Sanjay Jaiswal

Engineering

Problems faced by youth

Challenges for today's youth

1. It's very difficult to remain consistent in our work for a long period of time.
2. And one of the difficult challenges is social media or we can say mobiles or technology which keeps us busy in insignificant thing.
3. And most dangerous challenge is "expectations".
4. And another is taking failure as a lesson or we can say afraid of being failed or hurt.

5. We can't control our anger, and we think that by doing that everything will be in our control.
6. And to keep motivating ourselves throughout the process of achieving goal.
7. Handling the pressure in difficult time.
8. Overthinking and negative thoughts which ruins our every moment.

Expectations of youth

1. Majority of youth in today's generation want results without any hard work.
2. Today's youth want to get loved and sympathy.
3. We expect loyalty and commitment from our friends, our partner and even from a stranger but we will not do the same.
4. And we also expect not to get hurt in any situation.
5. our expectations are to live a good luxurious life.
6. We want to watch all the series and movies and even want to get every exam clear with a better grade.
7. We expect everything will go exactly as we are imagining in our virtual world.
8. We expect other person to act according to our likes/dislikes.

Mrunamayee Dadasaheb Gaikwad

12th Science

Youthhood is not a face of life, it is a state of mind, it is not a matter of rosy cheeks, red lips and supple knees, it is a matter of the will, quality of the imagination, vigor of the emotions, it is the freshness of the deep springs of life.

Youth is that community or group of people who are the future bearer of this country. They are widely outcast - they are neither considered too young to be pampered nor they old enough to take responsibility on their shoulders.

The young people are plagued with insecurities and doubts. Their way of living is challenged at every level - be it emotional, physical, academic or interpersonal relations. Problems are a sign that there is hope for innovation and a better tomorrow.

Value based proper education system should be a priority and everyone's birth right, but educational quality is discriminatory according to the financial status. In today's time youngsters with multiple degrees from prestigious institutes can get a well-paid job and live a decent lifestyle. With saturation of the organized sector, finding a job become difficult. This competitive environment makes people simply locked up in their jobs only as an income generator and nothing more. Furthermore, the internship doesn't help as it is not well regulated. The employers take advantage of the situation by putting a lot of work - load on interns and paying them low or not paying at all. This turns the journey of passionate experience into a heavy burden.

More than 30% of Indian youth are unemployed and not involved in any education or training. This is one of the major causes for poverty, juvenile delinquency, substance abuse, etc.

Failure of education system, is because of punishment is priorities over education. Schools and colleges are not able to educate and train the youth to compete with modern professional challenges, there is lack of motivation and creativity. We just tell the youth; how to do certain things and fail to lead by example. Today's youth doesn't plan for their future, lacking in proper decision making capabilities and tend to procrastinate. They think everything will fall into their hands just like in movies, and they can't accept the fact that it doesn't happens. Everything is easily available to today's youth, so they tend not to value the emotions and hard work behind it. Moral degradation in youth is the major problem that the society faces. If we reinstall moral values it will help us to reduce social problems like unrest, social erosion, crime, separatism, class conflict, isolation, lack of well-being and collective distance.

Thoughts bring forth actions, actions produce habits, while habits become character. Globally more than 264 million people of all ages suffer from depression and other mental stresses and problems. This are caused by many reasons, some of which are obesity, materialism, arguments, bullying, violence in school, early maturity, single parent household, peer pressure, etc. They cause social anxiety and discomfort; they riddle them with self - doubt and worthlessness. Such negativity must be overcome by positive emotions like passion, sympathy, patience, tolerance and peace, which most of today's youth lack. Children are likely to live up to what is believed of them, all they need is a little help and someone to believe in them.

These problems have become normal. When things become normal, they become accepted, and when they become accepted, they become expected.

Life is not defined by the bad choices that we made or will make, but by our willingness to give back more than we take.

Siddhi Sarang Modi
10th CBSE

Youth - not an easy stage of life.

Life ... It is, as we know, all about ups and downs, victories and failures, friends and enemies, love and hate, appreciation and devaluation but youthhood, the phase considered and believed conventionally, is crucial and vital in one's life. This nightmarish stage needs to be crossed with a bridge of understanding and acceptance. You find yourself at a place where two or more roads diverge but, wisely and discreetly you should to and must choose one which would help you to reach to your destination. It proves to be a turning point of your life. Crossing the bridge, who's beneath is wide and vast sea is, not at all easy. Peer pressure, friends, parents nagging, crushes, teachers' taunts, social medias, bullying, is inevitable. Being a youth, must face strong competition of gaining more marks than anyone else. We must digest several complications, even if they are expressible, ourselves. Rapidly changing world has been the major reason of change in the lifestyle of youth which seems difficult for parents to accept, this is called as generation gaps! Boards, considered as the milestones, must be tackled with changing and altering moods and behavior. At this stage, the hormonal change in us is difficult to adapt and have a successful victory over challenges. Parents consider us to be contemptible, rude, ill-behavioral, who has been spoiled by our friends. Aggression, hatred, irritation are some feelings which surge in us every now and then. We are seen to be pissed over one or the other. We want to be supported, encouraged, loved and be behind our back even if we are wrong, because ego is more important. Feeling of understanding is near to absent in us. Friends, girlfriends, boyfriends are most important. Using slangs, allowance to watch, do whatever we wish to, allowance to go wherever we want is an ideal day for us. Clothing's, brands, beauty, weight, height are vital for judging a person for us.

We cannot and should not be blamed for this. Being youth is not our choice, it is just a stage.

But yes, this is also the best stage of life. All our beauty, characteristics flourish at this stage. Being beautiful is much easier at this point of our life. Also, this is the step to our future, which we must pave during this stage.

Hence life is unavoidable and not easy!

Aditi Ramdas Salunke

11th Science

Challenges and problems faced by students during JEE preparation

I was happy and content for being a top student in my whole life. It had given me a kind of momentum to get going in my academics. Scoring 97% in the 10th was a bit disappointing, as I expected to be at 98%+, however was indeed a reason to cheers! Post this major milestone, I decided to take up the journey for my next major milestone, i.e. A dream to be in IIT's. I took the admission to one of the renowned coaching center for JEE coaching. This was the time, when I started interacting with many more JEE aspirants. Soon my routine has taken a full circle. I started feeling that all that we were taught was just irrelevant! My routine has become activities pivoted around preparation for JEE.

First couple of monthly tests were pleasing as I stood at good position among the group of highly talented students. I was least prepared to receive a shock when I gave my first test in JEE advance pattern. I came to home crying, after knowing my rank as it gone down to 100+ , I could barely make it to the premium batch, but with a lot of embarrassment!

Now that I have realised where I stands, I have started to consult my lecturers, friends and those who made to IITs with help of my contacts. Suddenly I found myself in an awkward situation where I started experimenting better ways to study every day. Strangely, I lost the plot. Neither I followed my proven method of study, nor could I follow others. Fully confused, I stepped back, introspected and carefully analyse the situation. Now I have adopted a new way of studying with a hybrid of my original method with some best practices of my friends. Hoping to have my studies improved in coming days…

Let me summaries my thoughts in two parts:

They say… IIT causes Intense Inner Transformation! In fact, I feel this starts a bit early during JEE preparation instead. Students at their adolescence, give up all the fun, mischiefs, joy and all other thing normally a person at their age enjoys, with an ambition to be an IITians. Their life revolves around this dream that after 2 years, they will enter their dream college and become successful in life. The amount of sacrifices students makes is enormous. For some the choice is their own, for others it is their parent's, peer's and relative's. Those who willingly to pursue JEE preparation are seen enjoying every interaction, discussion and debate. They take every problem as a new challenge and enjoy this process thoroughly. They follow success stories of ex-students and derive confidence from inspirational stories of IITians and its Alumni.

On the contrary those who has been pushed into the rat race by virtue of other's choice have tremendous pressure to perform, to be at top in every test. While their preference may be Sports, Music, art, or other academic streams, where they could be successful. The gap in expectations and performance take the toll on their ability to cope up with the pressure of fulfilling expectations. They tend to have low esteem and self-confidence. At time the student has to go through depression which is extremely difficult to overcome.

I am lucky to have a strong inclination towards preparations for JEE and least expectations from my parents and wish to be successful. My parents have always supported me in all my decisions and I have never felt any pressure from their side. If not, I am confident to make a cut to some good colleges and be successful. However, those pass this testament of JEE preparation have a huge transformation in their life. They are surely prepared for the challenges in life though failed in making a cut to the premium institutes.

I feel JEE preparation is worth aspiring for... but be thoughtful of sacrifices, pressure and hard work!

Raj Tarunkumar Jaiswal

Engineering

---

1) Today's Youth face the challenges to manage the pressure to succeed in every field of life and only few of them are aware of effective time management.

2) Today's Youth also face materialism which taught them to measure success and happiness in life based on how much stuff (collection of things or ideas) they have. It results in dissatisfaction and negativity in one's life.

3) One of the main challenges is to face bullying which is caused by the rise of using social media by youth which has made bullying more public.

4) Academic problems are also faced by the youth which involves getting drop out from college, clearing all the subjects of academic year, also to score marks and many more. Some of them feel so much pressure to get into college which is good for them and that they are burning themselves out before they graduate from college.

5) One of the major problem is also that, they feel loneliness. They wanted to be in company but some circumstances and feeling within them forces to be alone.

6) Also, some of the major challenges are Emotional Imbalances, Alcoholism and Drug Addiction, Suicidal Tendencies and many more.

OVERVIEW

Until now, you have gone through so much of reading. It's time to take a pledge that you will not see negative aspects of youngsters but would focus more on building positive narratives with belongingness. Once they realize, they will put extra efforts to change their life positively, ultimately will helps in nation building.

Youngsters start following this routine daily:

- Exercise, Yoga, Pranayama, Meditation
- Timely food that too Sattvik (enough vegetables, fruits, dry fruits)
- Read few pages to add new knowledge related to science, technology, law, economics, history, current affairs, philosophy, etc....
- Play on ground, no video games on mobile, computer
- Plan a day, quality time for study, activities, project or goal
- Give some time for music, creativity
- Spend quality time with parents, siblings
- Don't forget to show gratitude towards god, near and dear ones, society.

> *This is your life. This is your time.*
>
> *"Sing like no one is listening,*
>
> *Love like you have never been hurt,*
>
> *Dance like nobody is watching, and*
>
> *Live like it's heaven on Earth."*
>
> *"Life is like riding a bicycle. To keep your balance, you must keep moving."*
>
> *— Albert Einstein*

REFERENCES

- https://www.bustle.com/articles/137865-8-reasons-meat-is-bad-for-you-yes-even-chicken
- https://www.mayoclinic.org/diseases-conditions/suicide/symptoms-causes/syc-20378048
- https://greatergood.berkeley.edu/article/item/how_gratitude_changes_you_and_your_brain
- https://www.helpguide.org/articles/addictions/drug-abuse-and-addiction.htm
- https://blog.firstcrayon.com/the-essential-guide-to-vedic-education-in-india-cedc2eeee0ea?gi=f7b86f4daf2c
- https://timesofindia.indiatimes.com/blogs/desires-of-a-modern-indian/the-importance-of-the-gurukul-system-and-why-indian-education-needs-it/
- https://www.inspirationalife.com/inspirational-and-motivational-stories-with-moral/
- https://www.investors.com/news/technology/top-10-steve-jobs-achievements/
- https://www.spiritualresearchfoundation.org/spiritual-practice/spiritual-paths/what-is-spirituality/?gclid=CjwKCAjwgbLzBRBsEiwAXVIygJrAHNZuTVqapVTJ4qFmOqqVoASNJE7ro1TXeV6p26mvQ92iduzg-hoCEsEQAvD_BwE
- https://journals.plos.org/plosone/article?id=10.1371/journal.pone.0219468
- https://www.helpguide.org/articles/healthy-living/how-to-improve-your-memory.htm
- https://mymemorymatters.org/spirituality/
- https://www.powerofpositivity.com/9-signs-youre-letting-ego-run-life/

- https://heartfulness.org/en/what-is-meditation/?utm_source=google&utm_medium=cpc&utm_campaign=website%20traffic&utm_term=meditation&gclid=Cj0KCQjw09HzBRDrARIsAG60GP_zCKVRIqSLqqrACpcPEMF7Slo_coZyWbzl9nv_2RNJAQ7g_Djw3xEaAgu-EALw_wcB
- http://www.historydiscussion.net/history-of-india/12-major-qualities-of-shivaji-explained/2864
- http://knowstartup.com/2017/03/10-success-lessons-from-ratan-tata/
- www.erinpavlina.com
- https://motivationgrid.com/steve-jobs-rules-for-success/
- https://www.investors.com/news/technology/top-10-steve-jobs-achievements/
- http://asiteducation.com/apj-abdul-kalam-life-and-achievements/
- https://myhero.com/pele2_dnhs_US_2011_ul
- https://www.kreyonmedia.com/post/?p=1412
- www.nelsonmandela.org
- www.nps.gov

9 789390 169016